Why Do Countries Export Fakes?

THE ROLE OF GOVERNANCE FRAMEWORKS, ENFORCEMENT AND SOCIO-ECONOMIC FACTORS

This work is published under the responsibility of the Secretary-General of the OECD. The opinions expressed and arguments employed herein do not necessarily reflect the official views of the OECD member countries or the European Union Intellectual Property Office.

This document, as well as any data and any map included herein, are without prejudice to the status of or sovereignty over any territory, to the delimitation of international frontiers and boundaries and to the name of any territory, city or area.

Please cite this publication as:
OECD/EUIPO (2018), *Why Do Countries Export Fakes?: The Role of Governance Frameworks, Enforcement and Socio-economic Factors*, OECD PublishingEUIPO, Paris.
https://doi.org/10.1787/9789264302464-en

ISBN 978-92-64-30245-7 (print)
ISBN 978-92-64-30246-4 (PDF)

European Union Catalogue number
TB-04-18-001-EN-C (Print)
TB-04-18-001-EN-N (PDF)

ISBN 978-92-9156-258-9 (Print)
ISBN 978-92-9156-257-2 (PDF)

The statistical data for Israel are supplied by and under the responsibility of the relevant Israeli authorities. The use of such data by the OECD is without prejudice to the status of the Golan Heights, East Jerusalem and Israeli settlements in the West Bank under the terms of international law.

Foreword

Trade in counterfeit and pirated goods poses a serious and growing risk to economic growth, undermining good governance, the rule of law and citizens' trust in government.

In order to provide policy makers with reliable empirical evidence about this threat, the OECD and the European Union Intellectual Property Office (EUIPO) joined forces to develop an understanding of the scale and magnitude of the problem. The results published in previous reports, *Trade in Counterfeit and Pirated Goods: Mapping the Economic Impact* (2016), *Mapping the Real Routes of Trade in Fake Goods* (2017) and *Trade in Counterfeit Goods and Free Trade Zones: Evidence From Recent Trends* (2018), show that trade in counterfeit and pirated goods amounted to up to 2.5% of world trade in 2013. Counterfeit and pirated products originate from virtually all economies on all continents, although middle-income and emerging economies tend to be relatively prominent players.

This report offers an opportunity to analyse in depth these findings to assess what are the drivers that will make an economy more likely to become active in the trade in fake goods. This can help in designing efficient policy responses to close the governance gaps. The results show that governance, production facilities, the existence of free trade zones, as well as the way that trade facilitation policies are implemented, are all factors that affect an economy's propensity to trade in counterfeit goods.

The study was co-ordinated by the Secretariat of the Task Force on Countering Illicit Trade, under the OECD High Level Risk Forum, which focuses on evidence-based research and advanced analytics to assist policy makers in mapping and understanding the market vulnerabilities exploited and created by illicit trade.

The quantitative research in this study relied on the rich global database on customs seizures provided by the World Customs Organization (WCO) and supplemented with regional data submitted by the European Commission's Directorate-General for Taxation and Customs Union, the US Customs and Border Protection Agency and the US Immigration and Customs Enforcement.

Acknowledgements

This report was prepared by the OECD Public Governance Directorate led by Marcos Bonturi in co-operation with the European Union Intellectual Property Office.

The report was prepared by Piotr Stryszowski, Senior Economist, and Florence Mouradian, Economist, jointly with Michał Kazimierczak, Economist at the European Observatory on Infringements of Intellectual Property Rights of the EUIPO, under the supervision of Stéphane Jacobzone, Deputy Head of Division, OECD and Nathan Wajsman, Chief Economist, EUIPO.

The authors are grateful to participants of several seminars and workshops for the valuable assistance provided. Special expressions of appreciation are due to Julio Bacio Terracino Deputy Head of the Public Sector Integrity Division at the OECD, Nikolaus Thumm at the European Commission Joint Research Centre, and Mary-Anne Venables, economic advisor at the UK Intellectual Property Office. The authors would also like to thank Ariadna Anisimov from the OECD Public Governance Directorate; John Koeppen from the US Patent and Trademak Office; Martin Johnson from the International Trade Administration, US Department of Commerce; Pierfrancesco Sanzi from the Italian Delegation to the OECD and Susan Wilson, US IP Attaché to the EU for their valuable insights.

The OECD Secretariat wishes to thank Liv Gaunt, Fiona Hinchcliffe and Andrea Uhrhammer for their editorial and production support.

The authors express their gratitude to the World Customs Organization (WCO), the European Commission's Directorate-General for Taxation and Customs Union, the US Customs and Border Protection Agency and the US Immigration and Customs Enforcement for their data and invaluable support.

Table of contents

Tables

Figures

Boxes

Acronyms and abbreviations

FTZ	Free-trade zone
GDP	Gross domestic product
GTRIC	General Trade-Related Index of Counterfeiting
HDI	Human Development Index
IP	Intellectual property
IPR	Intellectual property rights
LPI	Logistics Performance Index
TFI	Trade Facilitation Indicator
WCO	World Customs Organization

Follow OECD Publications on:

http://twitter.com/OECD_Pubs

http://www.facebook.com/OECDPublications

http://www.linkedin.com/groups/OECD-Publications-4645871

http://www.youtube.com/oecdilibrary

http://www.oecd.org/oecddirect/

Executive summary

Trade in counterfeit goods is a longstanding – and growing – socio-economic threat to effective governance, efficient business and the well-being of consumers worldwide, and is becoming a key source of income for organised criminal groups. It also damages the engine of economic growth, by reducing firms' revenues and undermining their incentives to innovate.

Existing empirical studies, including the recent OECD-EUIPO studies *Trade in Counterfeit and Pirated Goods: Mapping the Economic Impact* and *Mapping the Real Routes of Trade in Fake Goods,* have found that counterfeit and pirated products originate from virtually all economies on all continents, although their intensity of involvement varies. Some tend to be important producers or transit points in trade in fake goods, while their neighbours play only marginal roles.

This report seeks to answer the question of why some economies are more involved than others. It draws on large datasets to quantify the various socio-economic conditions that determine an economy's propensity to become an active actor in the trade in fake goods. The analysis finds five main drivers:

1) **Governance**: high levels of corruption and poor intellectual property protection are factors that greatly influence the degree of exports of fake goods from an economy.

2) **Free trade zones (FTZs):** FTZs offer a relatively safe environment for counterfeiters, with good infrastructure and limited oversight. The share of fake goods from economies hosting the 20 biggest FTZs is twice as big as from economies that do not host any FTZs.

3) **Production facilities:** low labour costs and poor labour market regulations are important drivers of trade in counterfeit and pirated goods. Improving working conditions, by raising the minimum wage or increasing paid leave, would decrease the share of counterfeit and pirated products exported, especially by economies with weak governance.

4) **Logistics capacities and facilities**: the ability to trace and track consignments is the key factor for reducing the share of counterfeit and pirated products in exports. However, other factors increase this trade, including low shipping charges; fast, simple and predictable customs formalities; and good quality trade and transport-related infrastructure (e.g. ports, railroads, roads and information technology). These factors tend to be also much more important drivers in economies that are highly corrupt.

5) **Trade facilitation policies**: The way trade facilitation is implemented matters. Enhancing transparency is likely to reduce the likelihood that an economy will export fakes: this includes the availability of detailed information on trade flows; the degree of involvement of an economy in the trade community; transparent and regular review of fees and charges imposed on imports and exports; and sound internal co-operation between border agency and other government units. Other factors tend to encourage

counterfeit trade, such as advance rulings (i.e. where the administration asks traders about the classification, origin, valuation methods etc. applied to specific traded goods), and the possibility to appeal administrative decisions by the border agencies. Importantly, the factors that potentially encourage counterfeit trade tend to be particularly pronounced in highly corrupt economies.

Of these five drivers, gaps in governance, especially high levels of corruption and gaps in intellectual property rights enforcement, are the crucial factor for trade in fakes, multiplying the effects of FTZs, logistic facilities or trade facilitation policies. The presence of FTZs is a particularly strong driver of trade in counterfeit and pirated goods in economies with weak governance, high corruption levels and a lack of intellectual property rights (IPR) enforcement.

While all the factors identified above matter, it is important to note that none of these factors *alone* can explain the intensity of exports of fakes from a given economy – it is the combination of numerous factors that allows important nodes in counterfeit trade to emerge. Also important to note is that many of the factors presented above can actually be extremely beneficial for trade in general, such as good logistics facilities. It is the *misuse* of these facilities that can result in higher flows of trade in fake goods. The degree to which this misuse occurs greatly depends on governance issues, particularly levels of corruption and IPR enforcement. The policy challenge is to reduce the scope for misuse, while keeping open the possibility of benefiting from trade.

1. Introduction. Trade in fakes: what do we know so far?

Counterfeiters tend to ship infringing products via complex trade routes in order to cover their tracks. Consequently, counterfeit and pirated products can be found in trade flows originating from virtually all the world's economies, though intensities vary. This chapter describes the existing research on the economies involved in the global trade in counterfeit and pirated goods.

Illicit trade in counterfeit and pirated goods[1] is a worldwide risk that keeps growing in scope and magnitude. Globalisation, trade facilitation and the rising economic importance of intellectual property (IP) have been fuelling economic growth on the one hand, while on the other opening up new opportunities for criminal networks to expand the scope and scale of their operations, with serious negative consequences for the economy and society. Trade in counterfeitand pirated goods also undermines good governance, the rule of law and citizens' trust in government, and can ultimately threaten political stability.

In order to improve the factual understanding of counterfeit and pirated trade, and to provide evidence for policymakers to formulate policies, the OECD and the European Union Intellectual Property Office (EUIPO) together carried out a comprehensive economic assessment of the problem (OECD/EUIPO, 2016[1]) and helped to identify key provenance economies of IP-infringing goods (OECD/EUIPO, 2017[2]). These studies have found that imports of counterfeit and pirated goods were worth USD 461 billion in 2013, or around 2.5% of global trade (OECD/EUIPO, 2016[1]), and that some provenance economies are more important sources of counterfeit and pirated products than others, either as key producers or strategic points of transit (OECD/EUIPO, 2017[2]).

This report completes these previous analyses by emphasising the country-specific drivers of trade in counterfeit and pirated goods – that is, the observable patterns that can explain why some countries emerge as key producers or hubs in the global trade of IP-infringing goods.

1.1. Where do we source our information?

All information concerning trade in counterfeit and pirated trade comes from the OECD-EUIPO database on customs seizures (OECD/EUIPO, 2016[1]) (see Box 1.1 for more details).

The descriptive analysis of the dataset of customs seizures presented in the OECD-EUIPO study identified 173 provenance economies of counterfeit and pirated products (OECD/EUIPO, 2016[1]). The study also noted that some of these provenance economies are more important sources of infringing goods than others. This could be because they are important producers of IP-infringing goods or because they are strategic transit points. In addition, some provenance economies may specialise in certain types of goods, modes of transport, etc.

The difficulty of determining whether a given economy produces counterfeit goods, or is a point of transit, has resulted in the coining of the term "provenance economy". This term was used in the OECD-EUIPO report (2016) following the OECD methodology developed in 2008.

Box 1.1. The OECD-EUIPO database on seized counterfeit and pirated products

The database on customs seizures is the critical quantitative input to this study. This database brings together data from three separate datasets from the World Customs Organization (WCO), the European Commission's Directorate-General for Taxation and Customs Union (DG TAXUD) and the US US Customs and Border Protection Agency (CBP). The database includes detailed information on seizures of IP-infringing goods made by customs officers in 99 economies around the world between 2011 and 2013. For each year, there are more than 100 000 observations in the database; in most cases, each individual observation corresponds to one customs seizure.

The database contains a wealth of information about IP-infringing goods that can be used for quantitative and qualitative analysis. In most cases, for each seizure the database details: the date of seizure, the mode of transport of the fake products, the departure and destination economies, the general statistical category of the goods seized and a detailed description of the goods, the name of legitimate brand owner, the number of products seized and their approximate value.[2]

A provenance economy is an economy detected and registered by a reporting customs agency as a source of an item that has been intercepted in violation of an IP right, whatever the amount or value concerned. Put differently, a provenance economy refers to both those economies of origin where the actual production of infringing goods is taking place, as well as those economies that function as ports of transit through which infringing goods pass on route to the destination economy.[3]

Lastly, the analysis carried out in the present study has highlighted an importnant measurement and data-related issue. Even though the information on counterfeit and pirated trade has improved significantly in recent years, more could be done to improve and expand information on this phenomenon within the EU. This is because even though some customs data identify a set of EU member countries as being provenance economies, these data refer in most cases to the points of entry of fake goods to the EU. Consequently the information on the production of fakes within the EU for the internal market and on the circulations of fakes within the EU is less precise; thus, conclusions that refer to EU countries are likely to be underestimated.

1.2. What has our research told us so far?

Figure 1.1 reports the top 25 provenance economies of counterfeit and pirated products seized by EU and US customs over the period 2011-2013. As mentioned in OECD/EUIPO (2016)[1], Asian economies are the largest exporters of counterfeit and pirated goods in terms of value, with the People's Republic of China and Hong Kong (China) at the top of the list.

Figure 1.1. Top 25 provenance economies of counterfeit and pirated products shipped to the EU and US, 2011-2013

Share of total seized value of IP-infringing products by US and EU customs

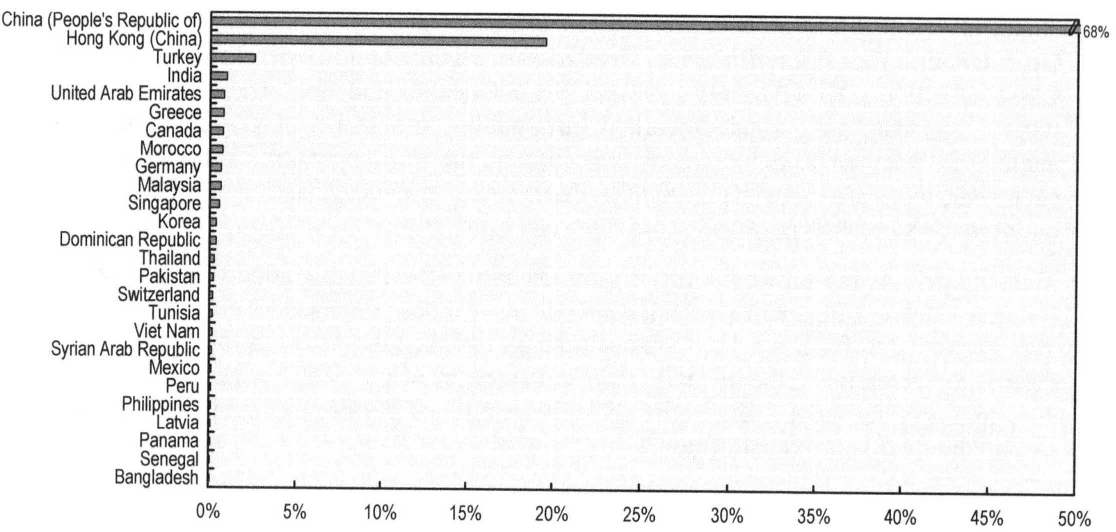

Drawing on this database of customs seizures of IP-infringing products, the OECD-EUIPO (2016) study developed a methodology, the General Trade-Related Index of Counterfeiting (GTRIC), which made it possible to measure the value of global trade in counterfeit and pirated goods (OECD/EUIPO, 2016[1]). The GTRIC methodology has also made it possible to both identify the key provenance economies for counterfeit imports around the world and to estimate the ceiling values of counterfeit and pirated products globally imported from those economies.

The OECD/EUIPO (2016)[1] report concluded that international trade in counterfeit and pirated products represented up to 2.5% of world trade in 2013, and was worth as much as USD 461 billion. Counterfeit and pirated products can be found worldwide and be shipped from all continents. However, some provenance economies are more important sources of counterfeit and pirated products than others.

Asian economies have been identified as the largest exporters of counterfeit and pirated products, both in absolute terms – see OECD/EUIPO (2017)[2] and Figure 1.1 – and in relative terms. This is shown in Figure 1.2, which lists the top 25 provenance economies in the global trade in fake goods in terms of the share of their exports that are counterfeit or pirated. In 2013, 10.1% and 8.7% of global exports from Hong Kong (China) and China, respectively, were counterfeit or pirated. These were followed by Pakistan (7.9%), Cambodia (6.3%) and Turkey (6.0%).

Figure 1.2. Top 25 provenance economies of counterfeit and pirated products in relative terms, 2013

As a share of world exports from each provenance economy

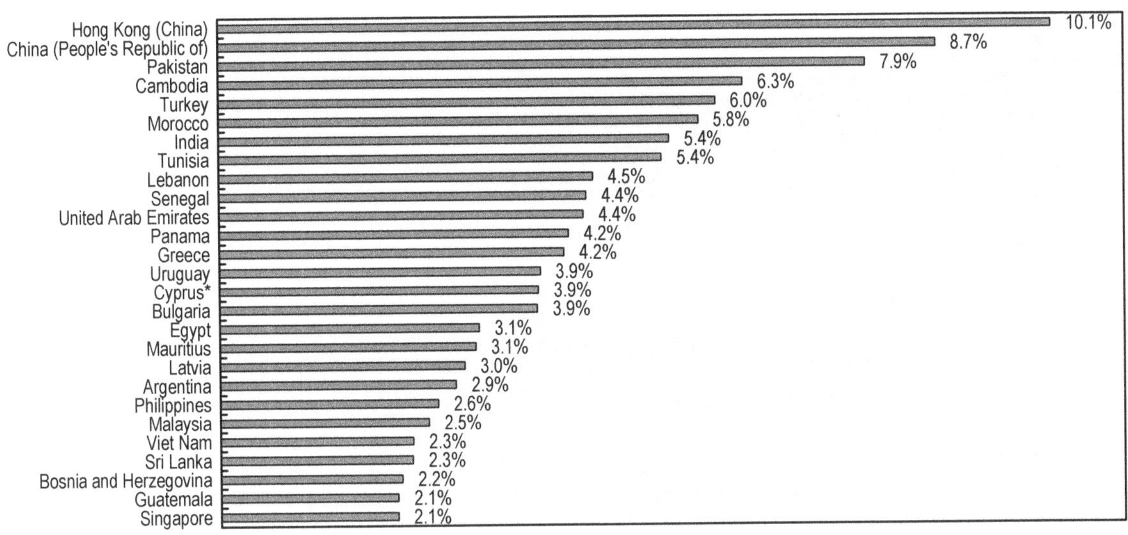

Source: Authors' own calculations based on OECD/EUIPO (2016)[1].

Focusing on the ten main product types which are particularly vulnerable to counterfeiting, the OECD/EUIPO (2017)[2] report explored the complex routes through which counterfeit and pirated goods are traded. They found that some of the main provenance economies of counterfeit and pirated products are important producers, while others are strategic points of transit.

Table 1.1 below lists the main producers of IP-infringing products shipped worldwide during the period 2011-2013. Clearly, China, India and Turkey were the key producers of counterfeit and pirated products, both in terms of value and the diversity of fake goods produced. The OECD/EUIPO (2017)[2] report noted however that China was the largest producer of almost every type of counterfeit good traded worldwide, with the exception of pharmaceuticals, which were mostly produced in India.

Several East Asian economies, such as Cambodia, Indonesia, Malaysia, Thailand and Viet Nam, also produced a relatively large range of different types of counterfeit and pirated products, though not as diverse as the countries mentioned above, and with a lower value. Finally, North African economies, such as Algeria, Morocco and Tunisia, and some Central American economies, such as Guatemala, Honduras, Mexico, Panama and Peru, more often specialise in the production of one or two specific types of counterfeit goods.

Table 1.1. The main types of counterfeit products shipped worldwide and their producers, 2011-2013

Producers	Type of goods
Algeria	Electronic and electrical equipment
Armenia	Watches and jewellery; toys and games
Bangladesh	Clothing; optical, photographic and medical equipment
Cambodia	Articles of leather and footwear; electronic and electrical equipment; optical, photographic and medical equipment
China (People's Republic of)	Articles of leather and footwear; clothing; electronic and electrical equipment; optical, photographic and medical equipment; perfumery and cosmetics; pharmaceuticals; watches and jewellery; toys and games
Ethiopia	Foodstuff
Guatemala	Clothing
Honduras	Clothing
India	Articles of leather and footwear; clothing; electronic and electrical equipment; foodstuff; perfumery and cosmetics; pharmaceuticals; watches and jewellery; toys and games
Indonesia	Articles of leather and footwear; foodstuff; watches and jewellery; toys and games
Kenya	Foodstuff
Korea	Electronic and electrical equipment
Malaysia	Articles of leather and footwear; optical, photographic and medical instruments; perfumery and cosmetics; watches and jewellery; toys and games
Mexico	Clothing; electronic and electrical equipment; toys and games
Morocco	Articles of leather and footwear; electronic and electrical equipment; toys and games
Pakistan	Foodstuff; optical, photographic and medical equipment; perfumery and cosmetics; watches and jewellery; toys and games
Panama	Articles of leather and footwear; clothing
Peru	Clothing
Philippines	Articles of leather and footwear
Singapore	Electronic and electrical equipment; perfumery and cosmetics; pharmaceuticals
Thailand	Articles of leather and footwear; clothing; electronic and electrical equipment; foodstuff; optical, photographic and medical equipment; watches and jewellery; toys and games
Tunisia	Articles of leather and footwear
Turkey	Articles of leather and footwear; clothing; electronic and electrical equipment; foodstuff; optical, photographic and medical equipment; perfumery and cosmetics; watches and jewellery; toys and games
Viet Nam	Articles of leather and footwear; clothing; foodstuff; optical, photographic and medical equipment; watches and jewellery; toys and games

Source: OECD/EUIPO (2017)[2]

The OECD/EUIPO (2017)[2] report also investigated the role of strategic transit points in easing the trade in fake goods. This includes falsifying documents to camouflage the original point of departure; establishing distribution centres for counterfeit and pirated goods; and repackaging or re-labelling goods. In addition, while imports of counterfeit goods are, in most cases, targeted by local enforcement authorities, they are less empowered to deal with goods in transit, which means that counterfeit goods are less likely to be intercepted while in transit to the final destination.

Table 1.2 lists the main strategic transit points in the global trade of counterfeit and pirated products that were identified in the OECD/EUIPO (2017)[2] report.

Table 1.2. Main transit points in the global trade of counterfeit products, 2011-2013

Transit point	Type of goods
Albania	Articles of leather and footwear; optical, photographic and medical equipment; perfumery and cosmetics; pharmaceuticals
United Arab Emirates	Watches and jewellery; toys and games; foodstuff; clothing; articles of leather and footwear; perfumery and cosmetics; pharmaceuticals; electronic and electrical equipment
Armenia	Watches and jewellery; toys and games; articles of leather; footwear
Azerbaijan	Articles of leather and footwear; electronic and electrical equipment
Bahrain	Watches and jewellery; toys and games
Bosnia and Herzegovina	Articles of leather and footwear
Belarus	Perfumery and cosmetics; pharmaceuticals
Belize	Electronic and electrical equipment
Cameroon	Electronic and electrical equipment
Dominican Republic	Optical, photographic and medical equipment
Algeria	Electronic and electrical equipment; optical, photographic and medical equipment
Egypt	Articles of leather and footwear; perfumery and cosmetics; pharmaceuticals; electronic and electrical equipment
Hong Kong (China)	Clothing; electronic and electrical equipment; watches and jewellery; toys and games; articles of leather and footwear; optical, photographic and medical equipment; perfumery and cosmetics; pharmaceuticals
Honduras	Watches and jewellery; toys and games
Iran	Perfumery and cosmetics; pharmaceuticals; articles of leather and footwear; articles of leather and footwear; foodstuff
Kuwait	Articles of leather and footwear; optical, photographic and medical equipment; perfumery and cosmetics; pharmaceuticals
Lebanon	Watches and jewellery; toys and games
Macau (China)	Watches and jewellery; toys and games; articles of leather; footwear
Morocco	Articles of leather and footwear; optical, photographic and medical equipment; electronic and electrical equipment; watches and jewellery; toys and games
Mexico	Watches and jewellery; toys and games
Mongolia	Optical, photographic and medical equipment
Nigeria	Electronic and electrical equipment
Panama	Perfumery and cosmetics; pharmaceuticals; watches and jewellery; toys and games; electronic and electrical equipment
Paraguay	Watches and jewellery; toys and games
Saudi Arabia	Foodstuff; perfumery and cosmetics; pharmaceuticals; watches and jewellery; toys and games
Senegal	Articles of leather and footwear
Singapore	Watches and jewellery; toys and games; articles of leather; footwear; clothing; perfumery and cosmetics; pharmaceuticals; electronic and electrical equipment; optical, photographic and medical equipment
Turkey	Electronic and electrical equipment; optical, photographic and medical equipment; perfumery and cosmetics; pharmaceuticals
Ukraine	Foodstuff; watches and jewellery; toys and games; clothing; optical, photographic and medical equipment
Yemen	Foodstuff; perfumery and cosmetics; pharmaceuticals

Source: OECD/EUIPO (2017)[2].

Hong Kong (China), Singapore and the United Arab Emirates are the main transit points for fakes around the globe. These hubs are found to specialise in the repackaging of counterfeits that are taken from large shipping containers and placed into smaller postal and courier packages that are then sent onwards to all economies. They specialise in a wide range of counterfeit goods, such as foodstuff, perfumery and cosmetics, pharmaceuticals, leather articles and handbags, footwear, optical, photographic and medical equipment, electronic and electrical products etc.

In addition, there are some important regional transit points. Several Middle Eastern economies (i.e. Bahrain, Iran, Kuwait, Saudi Arabia, Yemen) are important transit points for trade in fake goods to Africa, and sometimes to the EU. Some economies function as exclusive transit points for shipments of counterfeits into the EU: Albania, Algeria, Armenia, Azerbaidjan, Belarus, Bosnia and Herzegovina, Mongolia, Morocco and Ukraine. Finally, numerous economies in Central America (e.g. Belize, Mexico, Panama) and the Caribbean (e.g. Dominican Republic) serve as transit points for counterfeit products en route to the US or South America.

To reiterate, available information suggests that virtually any economy in the world can be the provenance of counterfeit and pirated trade, either as a place that produces infringing goods or as a point of transit through which infringing goods pass. Of course some of these provenance economies are more important sources of infringing goods than others. This could be because they are important producers of IP-infringing goods or because they are strategic points of transit. In addition, some provenance economies can specialise in certain types of goods, or in certain modes of transport, etc. The following chapters present a fuller quantitative picture of counterfeit trade at economy level, and explore why the counterfeit profiles vary for economies that otherwise seem similar.

References

OECD/EUIPO (2017), *Mapping the Real Routes of Trade in Fake Goods*, OECD Publishing, Paris, http://dx.doi.org/10.1787/9789264278349-en.

OECD/EUIPO (2016), *Trade in Counterfeit and Pirated Goods: Mapping the Economic Impact*, OECD Publishing, Paris, http://dx.doi.org/10.1787/9789264252653-en.

Notes

[1] Goods that infringe trademarks, copyrights, patents or design rights.

[2] There are two principles for reporting the value of counterfeit and pirated goods: 1) declared value (value indicated on customs declarations), which corresponds to values reported in the general trade statistics; and 2) replacement value (price of original goods). The structured interviews with customs officials and the descriptive analysis of values of selected products conducted in OECD-EUIPO (2016)[1] revealed that the declared values are reported in most cases.

[3] This definition of "provenance economies" is used only in this study. It should not be confused with the definition used by the World Customs Organization, which uses the term "provenance" for the last economy that the goods passed through. See for example, www.wcoomd.org/en/topics/origin/overview/challenges.aspx.

2. Key drivers of trade in fakes

This chapter presents the quantitative investigation into the factors that determine economies' propensities to become active actors in the trade in fake goods. It determines five sets of indicators that shape economies' propensities to become important actors in this trade: production facilities, governance, free trade zones, trade facilitation policies and logistics capacities and facilities. In addition, poor governance (i.e. high levels of corruption and poor enforcement of intellectual property rights) was identified as a crucial element that amplifies the effects of other drivers.

As with any business, parties that engage in trade in counterfeit or pirated products do so to make profit. They therefore face the same worldwide market challenges as those faced by legitimate business (OECD, 2008[3]). If those market challenges are complex, they are in general largely dependent on an economy's characteristics, notably in terms of production, logistics and trade facilities, as well as the institutional environment.

In order to explain why counterfeiters and pirates are more engaged in global counterfeiting and piracy in some economies than others, we need to establish the country-specific drivers of trade in counterfeit and pirated goods. This report establishes some links between the share of counterfeit and pirated goods exported by each economy and indicators on its production, trade and logistic facilities, governance and measures of free trade zones. It also distinguishes between those characteristics that explain why some economies emerge as producers of fake goods, and those that explain why some economies emerge as key transit points.

The database built for this exercise covers 164 economies worldwide over the period 2011-2013. The analysis linked the share of fake exports in total exports estimated in the OECD/EUIPO (2016) report with a set of explanatory variables:

- production facilities (measured as the share of the manufacturing sector in value added, labour costs and labour market regulations)
- free trade zones (e.g. number of FTZs, employment and number of firms in FTZs)
- governance (e.g. indicators for corruption provided by the World Bank Governance Indicators, or index for irregular payments and bribes or intellectual property protection provided by the World Economic Forum)
- logistical performance (e.g. an index based on efficiency of the customs clearance process, competitively price shipments, quality of transport infrastructure);
- trade facilitation (e.g. index of disciplines on the fees and charges imposed on imports and exports, degree of internal co-operation between border agency and other government units).

Given that the dependent variable is expressed as a percentage (share of the value of counterfeit and pirated products exported by each economy in its total exports), this analysis uses a fractional logistic regression (Box 2.1) which is the standard approach for modelling this type of data.

Box 2.1. The fractional logistic regression

The most common method used in quantitative analyses is the ordinary linear regression (OLS). However OLS is not suitable in this case, as the main variable is distributed on a [0,1] interval. Put differently, in OLS the model can generate predictions outside the unit interval, that is, values below 0 or above 1 (Long, 1997[4]). The other problem is that the relationship is not linear but sigmoidal (S–linear in the middle, but flattened on the ends). Using a proportion in a linear regression model will generally yield nonsensical predictions for extreme values of the regressors.

Some researchers have also considered using censored normal regression techniques such as a tobit model on proportions data that contain zeros or ones. However, this is not an appropriate strategy, as the observed data in this case are not censored: values outside the [0,1] interval are not feasible for proportions data.

The usual approach for modelling this type of data structure is to use a fractional logistic regression. The canonical paper is the one by Papke and Wooldridge (Papke and Wooldridge, 1996[5]). The fractional response model implements quasi-likelihood estimators in order to predict the conditional mean of the share of counterfeit and pirated products exported by a given economy. The advantage is that there is no need to know the true distribution to obtain consistent parameter estimates (Papke and Wooldridge, 1996[5]). This means that the true model does not need to be, for example, a logit. If the true model is a logit, then fitting a logistic regression via maximum likelihood gives consistent parameter estimates and asymptotically efficient standard errors.

By contrast, if the conditional mean of the model is the same as the conditional mean of a logit but the model is not a logit, the point estimates are consistent, but the standard errors are not asymptotically efficient. The standard errors are not efficient, because no assumptions about the distribution of the unobserved components in the model are made. Thus the model developed in this study uses robust standard errors.

Formally, the dependant variable of the model is the annual share of counterfeit and pirated goods exported by economy i in year t and is denoted y_{it}. Statistics on these shares are presented in chapter 1. This continuous dependant variable defined in the interval [0,1] can be explained by the vector of explanatory variables x_{it}. The fractional response model fits a regression for the mean of conditional on x as follows:

$$E\left(y_{it}|x_{it}\right) = G\left(x_{it}\beta\right)$$

with the maintained assumption that for all it $G(.)$ is a known function satisfying $0 < G(.) < 1$ for all $z \in \mathbb{R}$. This ensures that the predicted values of y_{it} lie in the interval [0,1]. As typically done, $G(.)$ is chosen here to be a logistic function.

The set of explanatory variables x_{it} includes indicators concening governance and IP protection (Section 2.1), FTZs (Section 2.2), production facilities (Section 2.3); logitistic facilities (see Section 2.4) and trade facilitation (see Section 2.5). The results of the fractional response model are presented in the next section.

Table A.A2 in Annex A presents a set of results for the fractional response model using the share of counterfeit and pirated exports as the dependant variable for each economy over the period 2011-2013. In this table, only the sign of the coefficient can be interpreted.

The next paragraphs describe these results, and draw out additional highlights obtained from the fractional response model.

2.1. Governance indicators

Corruption, poor legislation of intellectual property and weak enforcement create favourable conditions for infringement activities. They help illicit trade to expand, both in the real and the virtual world, by altering the calculation of risks and rewards for counterfeiters and pirates in favour of multiple infractions and making the counterfeit products more widely available (OECD, 2017[6]).

Firstly, the legal and regulatory frameworks combating counterfeiting and piracy, particularly in terms of IP protection, are key institutional factors since they can have significant impacts on the behaviour of counterfeiters and pirates (OECD, 2008[3]). Legal systems provide rights holders with instruments to take action against parties that infringe on what is legally protected, and to claim compensation for the losses suffered as a result of the infringement (OECD, 2008[3]). Strong frameworks can deter illicit activity, while weak frameworks would effectively be viewed as permissive and encourage parties to engage in counterfeiting activities.

Secondly, laws and regulations can only affect the level of counterfeiting and piracy if they are enforced (OECD, 2008[3]). If the resources devoted to enforcement are inadequate, or if intellectual property rights are not otherwise enforced by the public authority, the value of the laws and regulations for the rights holders is diminished.

The level of corruption is particularly important in this regard since it undermines enforcement in several ways: illicit production facilities may go undetected if authorities choose to ignore them; distribution channels may be breached if fake goods are allowed to be mixed with genuine articles at various stages of distribution; or complaints may never be acted on if authorities effectively shelve cases (OECD, 2008[3]). In these circumstances, even the strictest law could therefore potentially fail to influence a party's decision to counterfeit/pirate, or not.

In order to demonstrate how the legal and regulatory frameworks (particularly for IP protection), enforcement and corruption affect counterfeiting activities, this study uses a set of governance indicators extracted from two well-known databases: the Worldwide Governance Indicators provided by the World Bank (Kaufmann, Kraay and Mastruzzi, 2010[7]) and the Corruption Perception Index administered by the World Economic Forum (Schwab and Sala-i-Martin, 2015[8]).

2.1.1. Description of data

Control of corruption

The first indicator related to corruption is the "control of corruption" ($wbgi_{cc}$) indicator, which is part of the Worldwide Governance Indicators provided by the World Bank (Kaufmann, Kraay and Mastruzzi, 2010[7]). These indicators are based on several hundred individual variables measuring perceptions of governance, drawn from 31 separate data sources constructed by 25 different organisations.

The particular aspect of corruption measured by the various sources differs somewhat, ranging from the frequency of "additional payments to get things done", to the effects of corruption on the business environment.

The "control of corruption" estimates are normally distributed with a mean of zero and a standard deviation of one for each year of measurement. This implies that virtually all scores lie between -2.5 and 2.5: the higher scores reflect better outcomes, i.e. less corruption (Kaufmann, Kraay and Mastruzzi, 2010[7]).

As mentioned above, a high level of corruption within an economy is likely to encourage parties to engage in counterfeit and pirated trade by undermining enforcement and lowering risks for counterfeiters and pirates. A first look at the data confirms this intuition. Figure 2.1 plots the share of counterfeit and pirated exports for each economy against its control of corruption score in 2013.

This cross-country comparison emphasises that, despite some outliers, the largest exporting economies of counterfeit and pirated products tend to score poorly for control of corruption (zero or below on the vertical scale), while economies with good corruption control are associated with a lower share of fake exports.

Figure 2.1. Share of fake exports and control of corruption, 2013

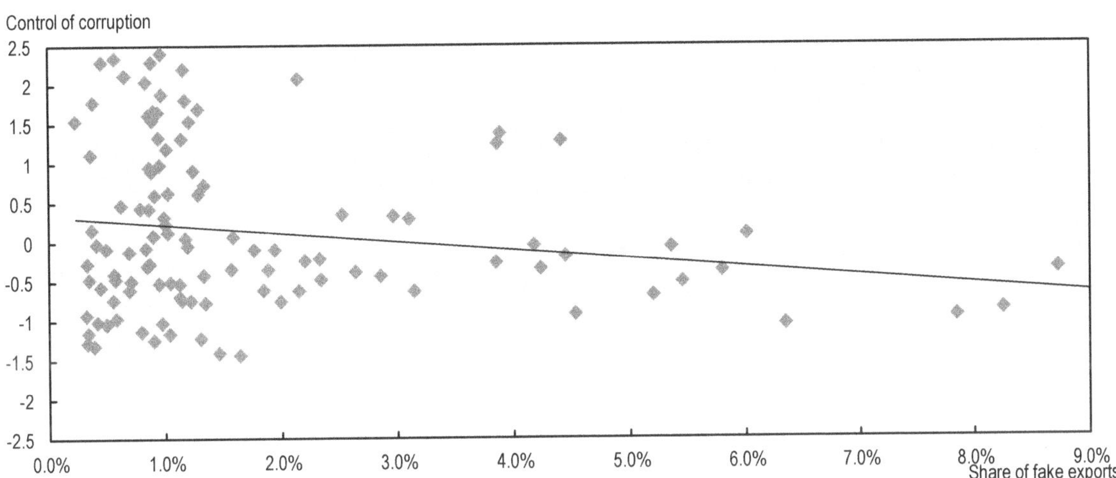

Notes: Each point corresponds to one economy. All corruption indicator scores lie between -2.5 and 2.5, with higher scores corresponding to better outcomes (less corruption).
Source: Authors' own calculations based on OECD/EUIPO (2016)[1] and Kaufmann, Kraay and Mastruzzi (2010)[7].

Irregular payments and bribes

In order to enhance the robustness of the results, this study also uses the index for "irregular payments and bribes" built from the Executive Opinion Survey administered each year in over 140 economies by the World Economic Forum (Schwab and Sala-i-Martin, 2015[8]). This survey captures the opinions of business leaders around the world on a broad range of topics for which data sources are scarce or, frequently, non-existent on a global scale.

The index for irregular payments and bribes is an average score across the five components of the following Executive Opinion Survey question: "How common is it for firms to make undocumented extra payments or bribes connected with (a) imports and exports; (b) public utilities; (c) annual tax payments; (d) awarding of public contracts and licenses; (e) obtaining favourable judicial decisions?" In each case, the answer ranges from 1 (very common) to 7 (never occurs).

Figure 2.2 illustrates that the largest exporters of counterfeit and pirated goods are economies where firms tend to make undocumented extra payments and bribes. On the other hand, numerous economies with a low perception index for irregular payments and bribes tend to export low levels of counterfeit and pirated goods. The results in Section 2.1.2 shed some light on the significance of this relationship.

Figure 2.2. Share of fakes and irregular payments and bribes, 2013

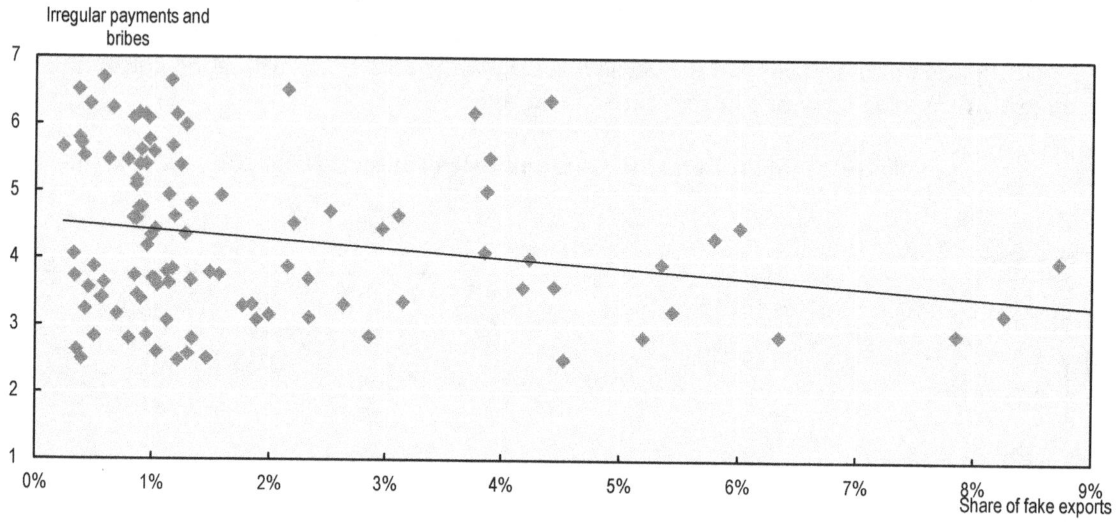

Notes: Each point corresponds to one economy. The indicator for irregular payments and bribes score from 1 (very common) to 7 (never occurs).
Source: Authors' own calculations based on OECD/EUIPO (2016)[1] and Schwab and Sala-i-Martin (2015)[8].

Intellectual property protection

In addition to corruption, the legal and regulatory frameworks for IP protection are another potentially key institutional factor for combating counterfeiting and piracy by having a significant impact on the behaviour of counterfeiters and pirates (OECD, 2008[3]). In order to check the accurancy of this effect, this study uses the index for intellectual property protection, also provided by the World Economic Forum (Schwab and Sala-i-Martin, 2015[8]). This is derived from the following Executive Opinion Survey question: "How would you rate intellectual property protection, including anti-counterfeiting measures, in your country?". Participants were asked to give a score between 1 (very weak) and 7 (very strong).

Importantly, the measures that report the strength of intellectual property rights regimes economy-wide do not need to be synonymous with the degree of counterfeiting and piracy in an economy, even though both phenomena are related (Box 2.2).

> **Box 2.2. Degree of IP protection and levels of counterfeiting and piracy in an economy**
>
> While a number of studies have examined the socio-economic effects of various degrees of IP protection, their results should not be directly applied to assessments of such impacts of counterfeiting and piracy. The impact that IP protection has on counterfeiting and piracy is nuanced and the existing indices of IP protection alone may not capture well the presence or absence of conditions conducive to exporting counterfeit goods. An economy with a strong IP regime could still be a major source of counterfeit and pirated items.
>
> This nuanced relationship between the IP protection indices and the degree of export of fake goods from a given economy arises because of at least three reasons. First, as studied in this report, export of counterfeit goods might require other conditions than lax IP protection, such as good transport and logistical facilities. Second, even economies with relatively strong legal IP regimes could fail to provide adequate enforcement for the prevention of export of fake goods. Their activity could focus, for example, on domestic counterfeiting and piracy. Third, an index of IP protection may capture the general quality IP-related framework, which can be important for certain effects, but omit dimensions of particular relevance to exports of counterfeit goods.

The results of the survey crossed against the estimates of counterfeit and pirated trade made by the OECD/EUIPO (2016)[1] for 2013 are plotted in Figure 2.3. Clearly, and despite the existence of some outliers, the share of counterfeit and pirated exports for economies with very weak intellectual property protection (scored 1 on the index for intellectual property protection) tends to be on average higher than for economies with strong intellectual property protection. The results in Section 2.1.2 confirm this relationship statistically.

Figure 2.3. Share of fakes and intellectual property protection, 2013

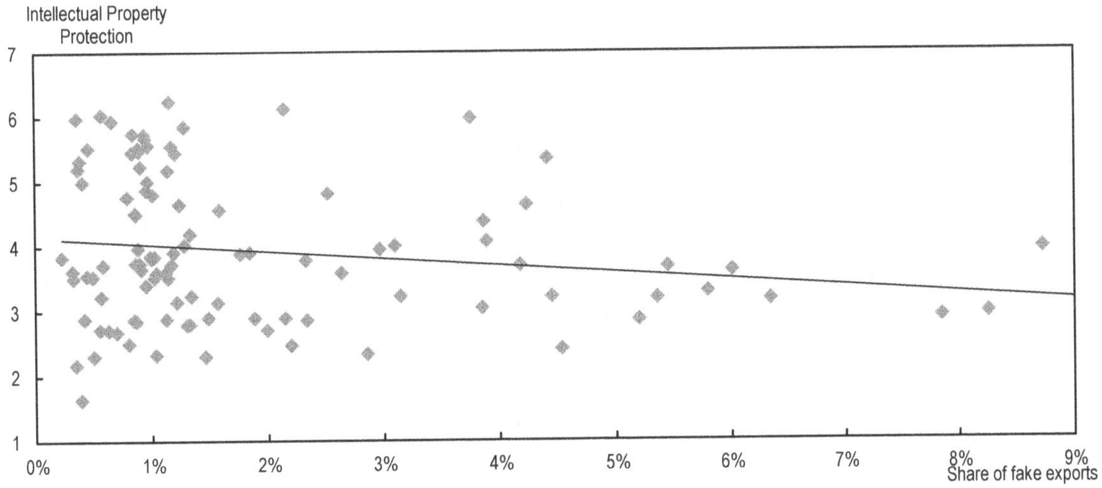

Notes: Each point corresponds to one economy. The indicator for intellectual property protection scores from 1 (very weak) to 7 (very strong).
Source: Authors' own calculations based on OECD/EUIPO (2016)[1] and Schwab and Sala-i-Martin (2015)[8].

2.1.2. Results

The results of the fractional logistic model first highlight that **the level of corruption and the quality of intellectual property protection are important drivers of counterfeit and pirated trade**. Concerning corruption, Table A.1 in Annex A shows that the share of counterfeit and pirated goods exports in total exports is significantly larger for economies where irregular payments and bribes are very common (columns 1 and 3) or where the control of corruption is very poor (column 4). This indicates that improving governance standards would significantly help to combat counterfeiting activities and piracy.

Secondly, columns (2) and (3) of Table A.1 indicate that the share of counterfeit and pirated exports is significantly lower for economies where intellectual property protection is very strong. This confirms that improving the legal and regulatory frameworks for IP protection would be a key institutional driver for reducing counterfeiting and piracy.

The magnitude of these impacts is illustrated in Figure 2.4, Figure 2.5 and Figure 2.6, which use the fractional response model to predict the conditional mean of the share of counterfeit exports according to the score for irregular payments and bribes, control of corruption and intellectual property protection, respectively. Figure 2.4 shows for instance that the share of counterfeit and pirated exports for economies where irregular payments and bribes are very common (rated 1 by the WEF score) is on average 3.5%, compared to only 0.7% for economies where irregular payments and bribes never occur (rated 7 by the WEF score).

Concerning the legal and regulatory frameworks of IP protection, Figure 2.6 shows that the share of counterfeit and pirated exports for economies where IP protection is very weak (rated 1 by the WEF score) is on average 3.9%, compared with only 0.7% for economies where IP protection is very strong (rated 7 by the WEF score). This means that weak IP protection within an economy tends to encourage counterfeiters and pirates to engage in global trade of fake goods.

Figure 2.4. Predicted share of fake exports depending on the frequency of irregular payments and bribes

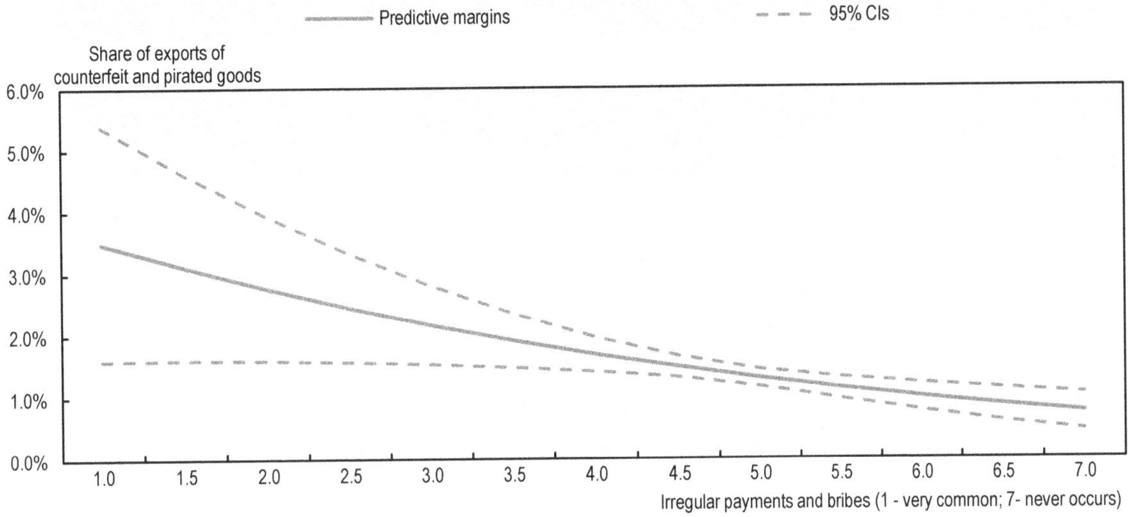

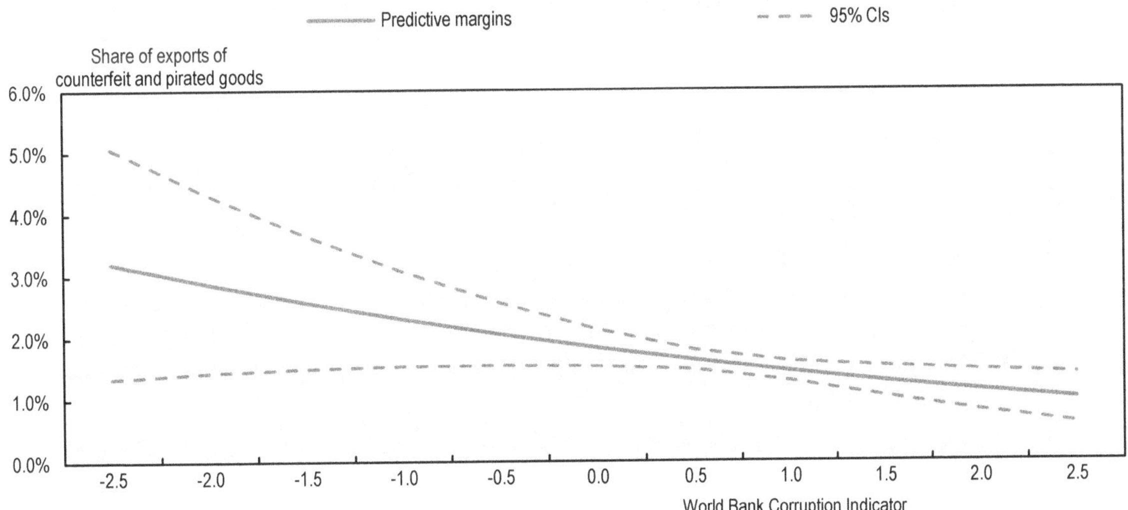

Notes: Calculations based on model 1 of Table A.1. "CIs" stand for "confidence intervals". The index of irregular payments and bribes was built on the following question: "how common is it for firms to make undocumented extra payments or bribes connected with (a) imports and exports; (b) public utilities; (c) annual tax payments; (d) awarding of public contracts and licenses; (e) obtaining favorable judicial decisions?" 1 = very common; 7 = never occurs.

Figure 2.5. Predicted share of fake exports depending on the level of corruption control

Notes: Calculations based on model 4 of Table A.1, Annex A. "CIs" stand for "confidence intervals". Control of corruption scores lie between -2.5 and 2.5, with higher scores corresponding to better outcomes.

Figure 2.6. Predicted share of fake exports depending on the quality of IP protection

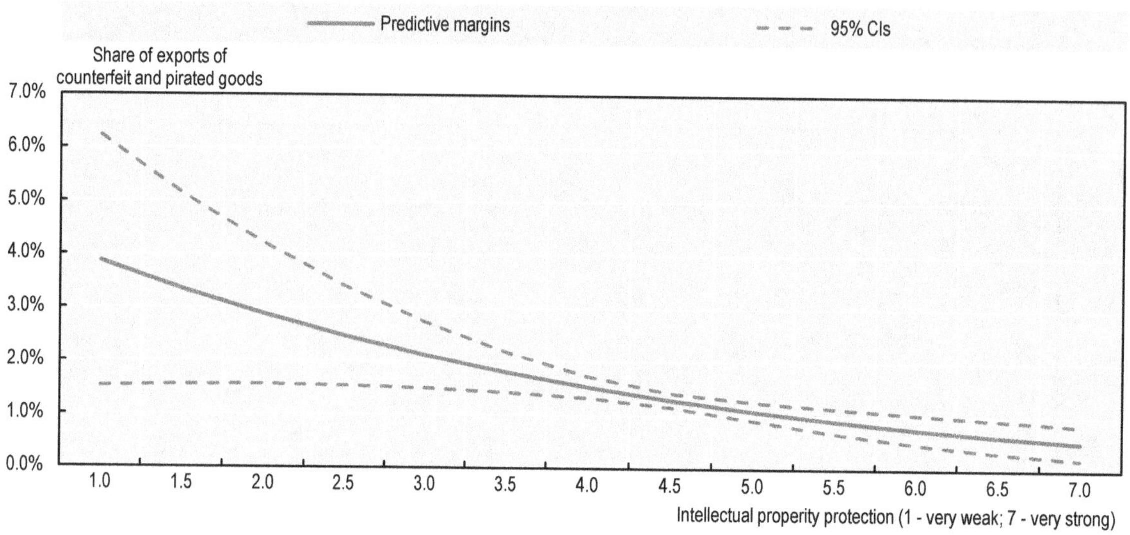

Notes: Calculations based on Model 2 of Table A.1, Annex A. "CIs" stand for "confidence intervals". The index for Irregular Payments and Bribes is an average score across the five components of the following Executive Opinion Survey question: how common is it for firms to make undocumented extra payments or bribes connected with (a) imports and exports; (b) public utilities; (c) annual tax payments; (d) awarding of public contracts and licenses; (e) obtaining favourable judicial decisions. In each case, the answer ranges from 1 (very common) to 7 (never occurs).

2.2. Free trade zones

In a recent report, the OECD/EUIPO (2018)[9] has highlighted that, while FTZs can provide unequivocal benefits to businesses and host countries, lightly regulated zones are also attractive to parties engaged in illegal activities, such as trade in counterfeit and pirated products or smuggling and money laundering. This is because these zones offer a relatively safe environment with good infrastructure and limited oversight.

2.2.1. Description of data

The OECD/EUIPO (2018)[9] study has already confirmed the links between FTZs and trade in counterfeit products. More specifically, it found clear links between the value of fake goods exported from an economy on the one hand, and the number of zones, number of firms operating in FTZs and the total value of exports from these zones on the other (OECD/EUIPO, 2018[9]).

These connections are illustrated in Figure 2.7, which plots the relationship between the share of fakes exported from each provenance economy in 2013 and their respective (a) number of free trade zones, (b) number of firms operating in FTZs, and (c) number of employees working in FTZs.

Figure 2.7. Share of fake exports and number and size of FTZs, 2013

(a) Number of FTZs

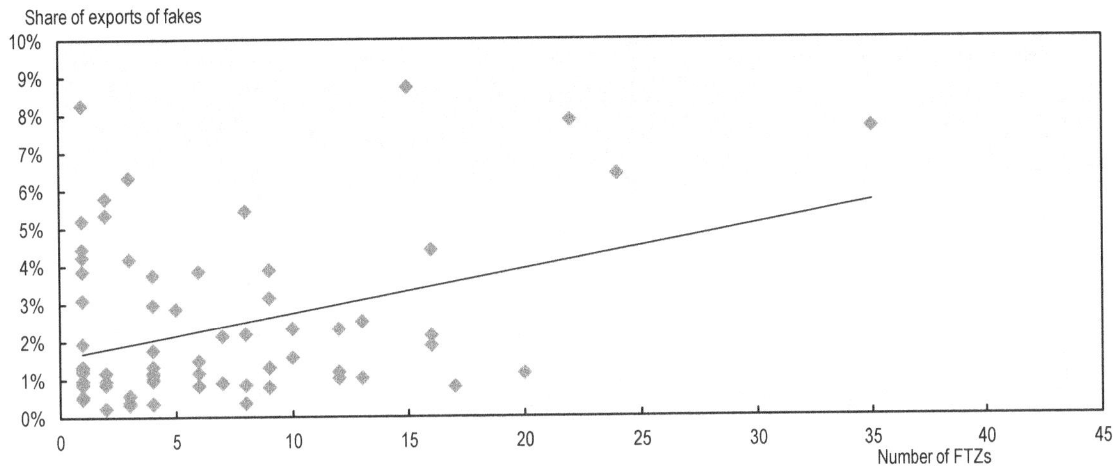

(b) Number of firms operating in FTZs

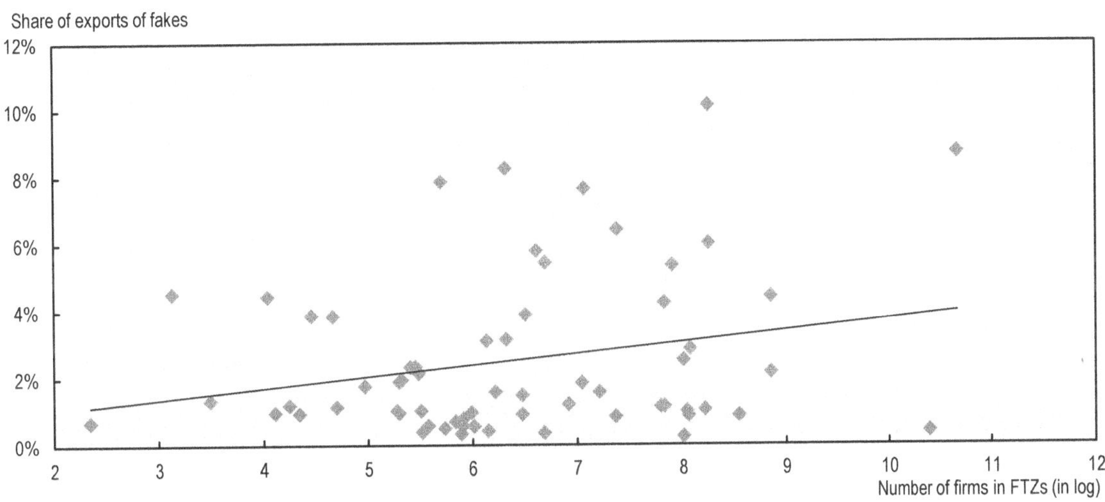

All these data on FTZs are extracted from the World FTZ Database, which brings together data from hundreds of academic resources, published papers and books, reports by international organisations, and documents on specific regions, countries and zones (Yücer, Siroën and Archanskaia, 2014[10]).

[1] In this database, FTZs are defined as zones with an export processing activity, which (a) involve the transformation of imported inputs; and (b) benefit from tariff exemptions under specific conditions that differentiate beneficiary firms from non-beneficiary firms.[2] For example, free ports, transit zones, "duty free" zones and zones eligible for other incentives (excluding tariff exemptions) were not included.

Figure 2.7 clearly indicates that the larger the number of FTZs, and number of firms and employees in a country's FTZs, the larger the share of counterfeit and pirated products in that economy's total exports. In other words, the larger the number and the size of FTZs within an economy, the more this economy is a source of counterfeit and pirated products in global trade.

(c) Employment in FTZs

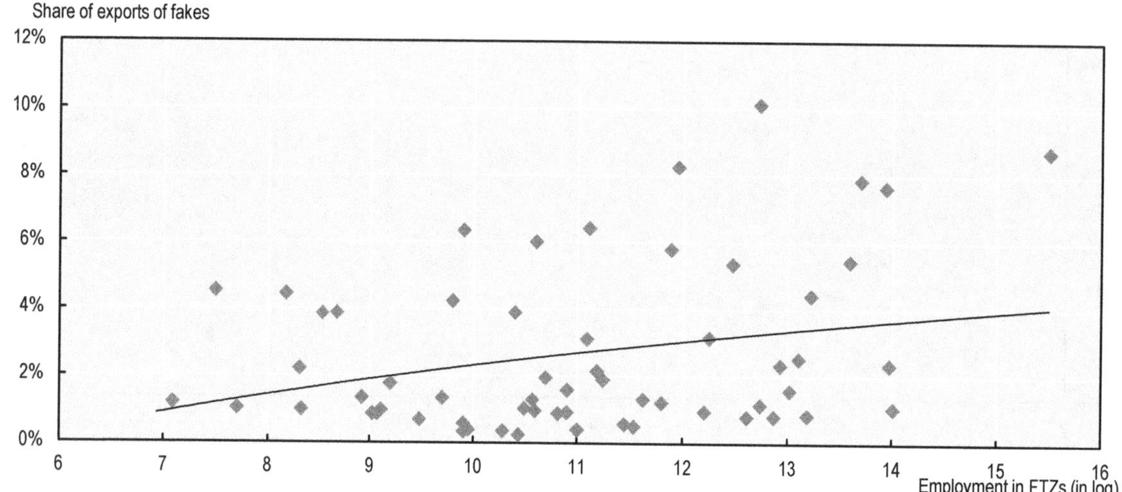

Source: Authors' own calculations based on OECD/EUIPO (2017)[9] and Yücer, Siroën and Archanskaia, (2014)[10].

2.2.2. Results

The results of the fractional response model confirm key insights from the OECD/EUIPO (2018)[9] study: free trade zones are important drivers of global counterfeiting and piracy. However, while the OECD/EUIPO study focuses on the value of counterfeit and pirated goods exported by economies, Table A.1 shows that establishing a new free trade zone also increases the host economy's share of counterfeit and pirated exports.

The magnitude of this impact is illustrated in Figure 2.8, which uses the fractional response model to predict the conditional mean of the share of counterfeit exports according to the number of FTZs within an economy. It indicates that, on average, **for economies not hosting FTZs the share in their total exports of counterfeit and pirated products (1.2%) is half the share for economies that host 20 FTZs (2.2%).**

Figure 2.8. Predicted share of fake exports depending on the number of FTZs

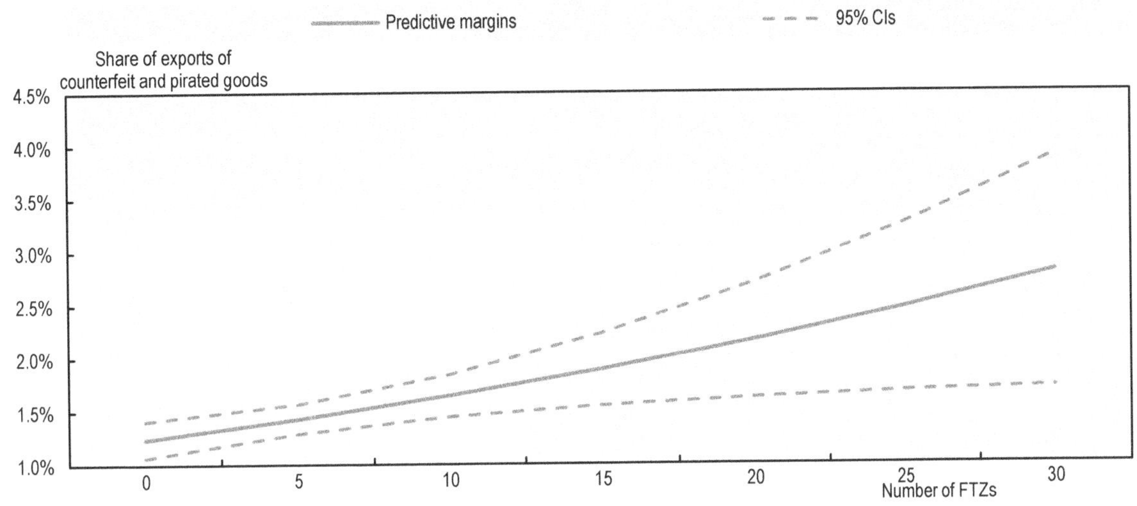

Notes: Calculations are made on the basis of column 1 displayed in Table A.1. "CIs" stand for "confidence intervals".

Another important result revealed by the model is that **FTZs are especially key drivers of trade in counterfeit and pirated goods in economies with weak governance**. This is illustrated in Figure 2.9, which shows that creating an additional free trade zone will raise the share of fake exports, especially for economies with a high level of irregular payments and bribes. On the other hand, the effect is nearly zero for economies where irregular payments and bribes never occur. This confirms that zones can be attractive to parties engaged in counterfeiting activities, especially when governments do not police them adequately.

2.3. Production facilities

Interest in counterfeiting or pirating a product depends in large part on the size of the market(s) that potentially can be exploited, and the unit profitability of the infringing items (OECD, 2008[3]). While this market potential is defined at the global level, the economic viability and the technical feasibility of the production of counterfeit and pirated goods largely depend on country characteristics.

2.3.1. Description of data

Regarding production facilities, the first hypothesis is that economies with a relatively developed manufacturing sector are likely to offer greater productive and technological capabilities for counterfeiters and pirates, leading to the likelihood of a higher scale of infringement activities. Figure 2.10 confirms this, revealing a positive relationship between the share of a manufacturing sector in value added and the share of counterfeit and pirated products exported by that economy in 2013.

Figure 2.9. Links between the number of free trade zones, corruption and the share of fake exports

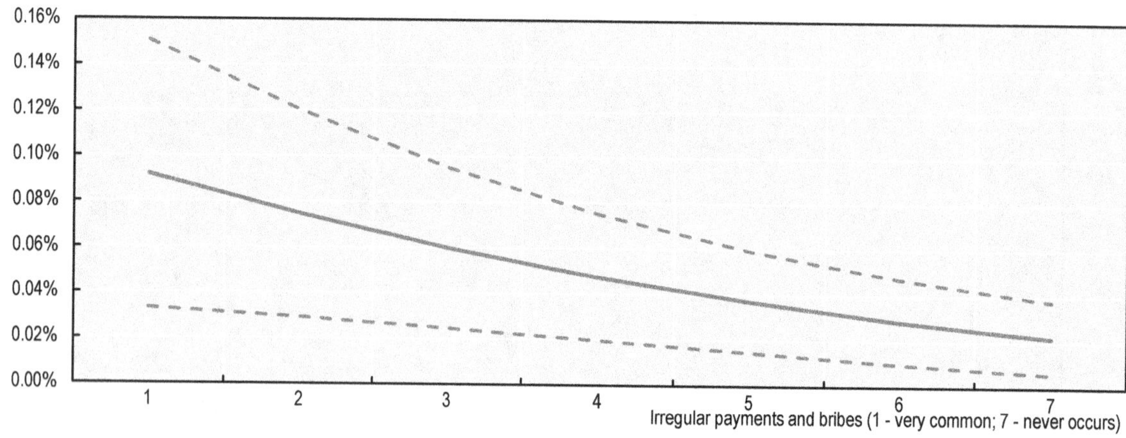

Notes: Average effect on conditional mean. "CIs" stand for "confidence intervals". Margins are calculated on the basis of column 1 displayed in Table A.1. The index of irregular payments and bribes was built on the following question: "how common is it for firms to make undocumented extra payments or bribes connected with (a) imports and exports; (b) public utilities; (c) annual tax payments; (d) awarding of public contracts and licenses; (e) obtaining favorable judicial decisions?" 1 = very common; 7 = never occurs.

Figure 2.10. Share of exports of fakes and share of the manufacturing sector in value added, 2013

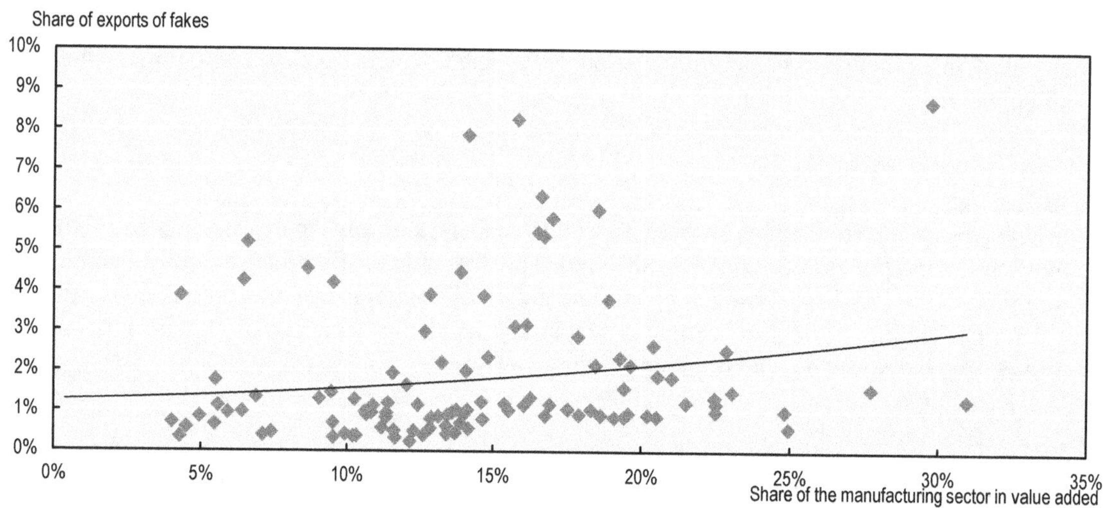

Note: Each point corresponds to one economy.
Source: Authors' own calculations based on OECD/EUIPO (2016)[1] and World Bank (2014)[11].

Given the illicit nature of counterfeit and pirated production and the necessity for counterfeiters and pirates to produce goods with high IP content at the lowest potential manufacturing costs, labour market regulations are also likely to be an important determinant of the magnitude of counterfeit and pirated exports produced in an economy. In order to test this relationship, this study quantifies the impact of some labour market indicators included in the World Bank's Doing Business Data (World Bank, 2014[11]) on the share of fake goods exported by an economy. The following paragraph first provides descriptive statistics on this relationship.

Concerning labour costs, economies with the lowest minimum wages (Figure 2.11) and those with a high ratio of minimum wage to value added per worker (Figure 2.12) tend to export relatively more counterfeit and pirated products than others. As indicators for the quality of labour market regulations are difficult to find, this study uses the number of paid days of annual leave (average for workers with 1, 5 and 10 years of tenure, in working days) as a proxy for working conditions in each economy. Figure 2.13 shows that economies offering less paid annual leave to workers also tend to export more counterfeit and pirated goods.

Figure 2.11. Share of exports of fakes and minimum wages for full-time workers, 2013

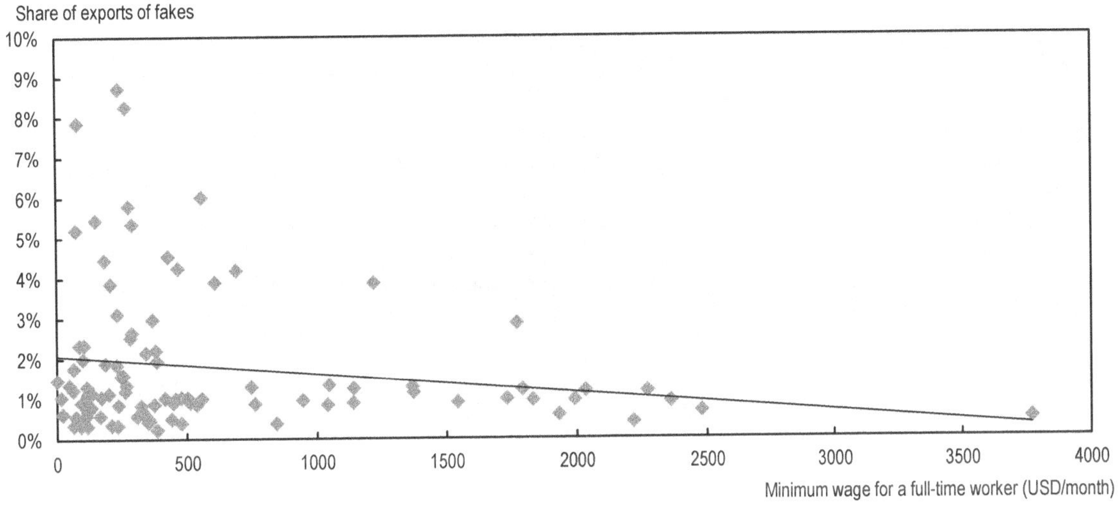

Notes: Each economy corresponds to one point. Data on minimum wages are for 2014.
Source: Authors' own calculations based on OECD/EUIPO (2016)[1] and World Bank (2014)[11].

Figure 2.12. Share of exports of fakes and ratio of minimum wage to value added per worker, 2013

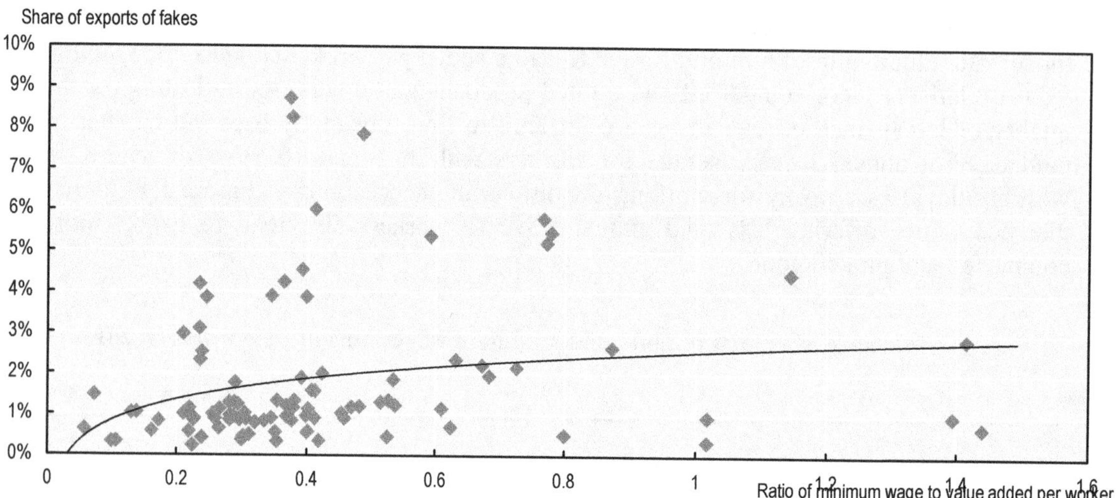

Notes: Each economy corresponds to one point. Data on the ratio of minimum wage to value added per worker are for 2014.
Source: Authors' own calculations based on OECD/EUIPO (2016)[1] and World Bank (2014)[11].

Figure 2.13. Share of exports of fakes and paid annual leave, 2013

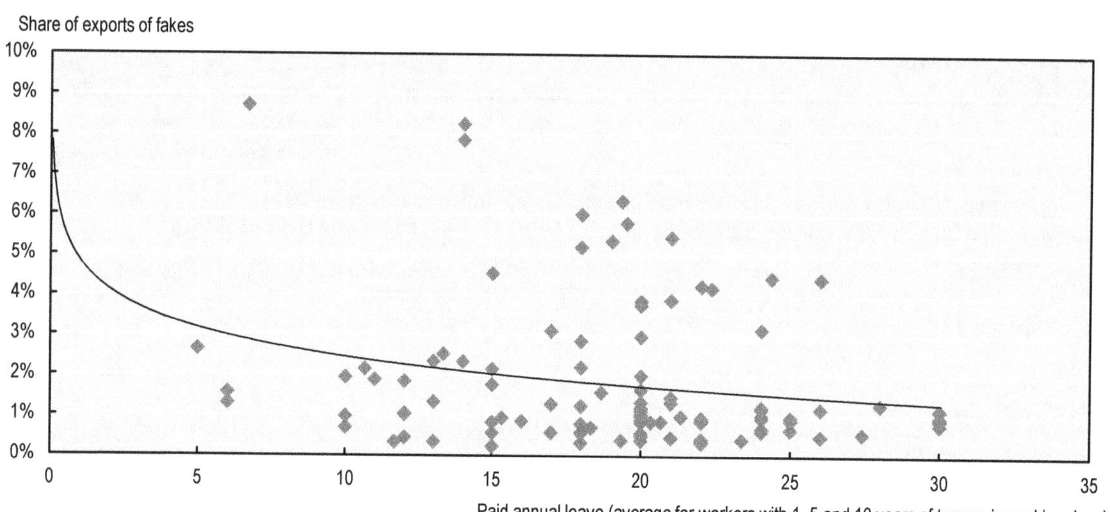

Notes: Each economy corresponds to one point. Data on paid annual leave are for 2014.
Source: Authors' own calculations based on OECD/EUIPO (2016)[1] and World Bank (2014)[11].

It should be noted that in many cases, the act of counterfeiting or piracy may not involve production. It may, for example, simply entail falsely labelling or packaging an item that otherwise did not violate an IP (OECD, 2008[3]). This would include, for example, marking a generic replacement brake part for an automobile to falsely indicate that the article was an OEM (original equipment manufacturer) branded item, or adding, without authorisation, a trademarked sticker to a product indicating that the product conformed to an industry standard. As discussed in OECD/EUIPO (2018)[9], free-trade zones serve as locations where items that are imported legitimately from one country may be repackaged in ways that violate IPRs, and then are exported to third countries. They are thus important drivers of trade in counterfeit and pirated goods, especially for key transit economies.

2.3.2. Results

Table A.1 in Annex A indicates that labour costs and labour market regulations are also important drivers of counterfeit and pirated trade. The four columns show that both a decline in the minimum wage and in the number of days of annual paid leaves significantly increases the share of counterfeit and pirated products exported by an economy. If both variables can be interpreted as proxies for the level of labour costs and the quality of labour market regulation respectively, it can be said that all other things being equal **economies with lower labour costs and poorer working conditions have larger shares of counterfeit and pirated exports**.

The value of this impact is illustrated in Figure 2.14, which plots the predicted share of counterfeit and pirated exports for an economy depending on the level of its minimum wage (left panel) and the number of annual paid leave days per worker (right panel). On average, the share of counterfeit and pirated exports for economies with only 2 days of annual paid leave per worker is 2.3%, compared with 1.5% for economies with 30 days of paid leave a year.

Figure 2.14. The links between fake exports and production conditions

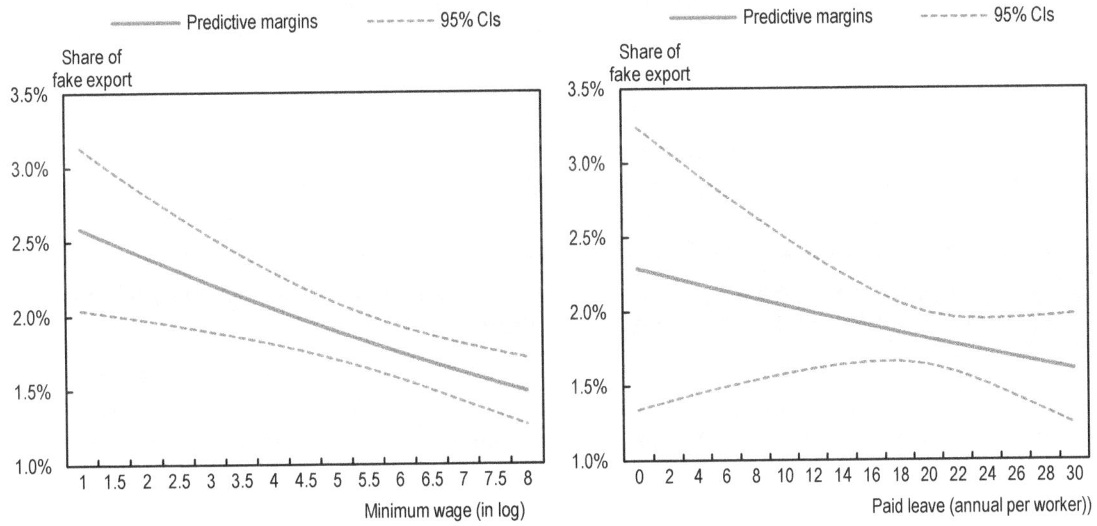

Note: Calculations are based on column 1 in Table A.1 in Annex A.

Another important finding of this exercise is that **an improvement of working conditions, as measured by a raise of the minimum wage or an additional day of paid leave, appears to decrease the share of counterfeit and pirated products exported, especially by economies with weak governance**. This is illustrated by Figure 2.15, which shows, for instance, that an additional day of paid leave would decrease the share of fake exports by 0.04 percentage points for economies with a high level of corruption (rated 1 on the index for irregular payments and bribes) and by only 0.01 percentage points for economies where irregular payments and bribes never occur (rated 7).

Figure 2.15. Impact on the share of fake exports of improving production conditions in a context of irregular payments and bribes

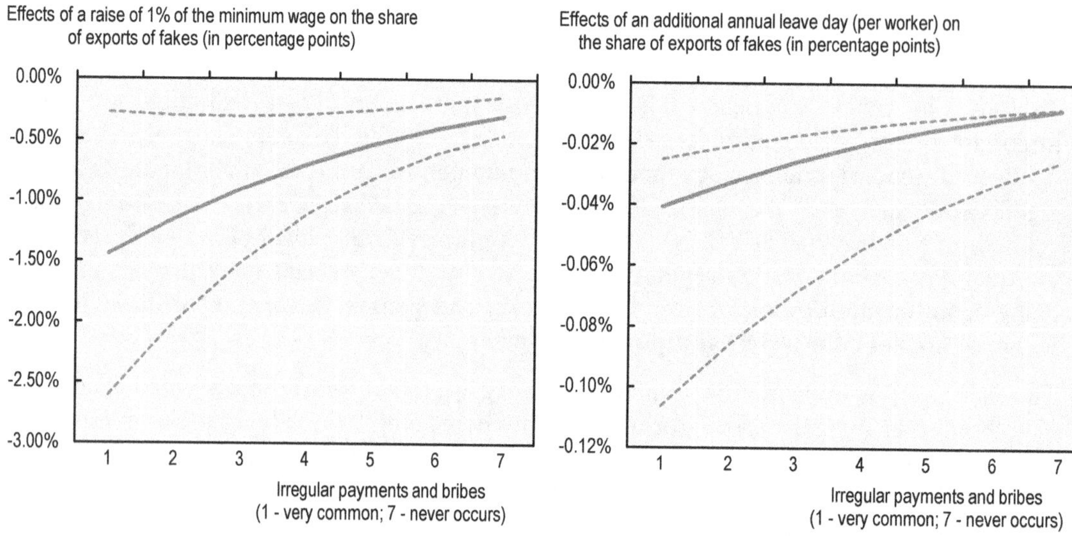

Notes: Average effects on conditional mean. "CIs" stand for "confidence intervals". Margins are calculated on the basis of model 1 displayed in Table A.1, Annex A. The index of irregular payments and bribes was built on the following question: "how common is it for firms to make undocumented extra payments or bribes connected with (a) imports and exports; (b) public utilities; (c) annual tax payments; (d) awarding of public contracts and licenses; (e) obtaining favorable judicial decisions?", where 1 = very common; 7 = never occurs.

2.4. Logistics indicators

Logistics are of particular relevance for trade in goods that infringe trademarks and copyrights. The ease of management of both inbound and outbound materials, parts, supplies and finished goods has an important bearing on the likelihood and extent to which a product is faked (OECD, 2008[3]). It is reasonable to assume, for instance, that the costlier and more complex the logistical management structure for bringing illicit goods to the market, the lower the likely level of infringing activity.

Efficient logistics might thus help to connect domestic counterfeiters and pirates to international markets through reliable supply chain networks (Arvis et al., 2016[12]). Supply chains are complex, but their performance is largely dependent on country characteristics, especially the soft and hard infrastructure and institutions that logistics require to operate well, such as imports, regulations, procedures, and behaviours (Arvis et al., 2016[12]).

2.4.1. Description of data

In order to explore if economies with efficient logistics export more counterfeit and pirated products than others, the study uses the Logistics Performance Index (LPI) provided by the World Bank and Turku School of Economics (World Bank and Turku School of Economics, 2018[13]).

The LPI is an interactive benchmarking tool conducted every two years; it ranks 160 countries on the efficiency of their international supply chains. It is based on a worldwide survey of logistics professionals on the ground who provide feedback on the logistics friendliness of the countries in which they operate and those with which they trade (World Bank and Turku School of Economics, 2018[13]).

LPI scores reflect professionals' perceptions of a country's logistics in terms of:

- the ability to track and trace consignments (*lpi_track*)
- the level of competence and quality of logistics services (e.g. transport operators, customs brokers) (*lpi_qual*)
- the ease of arranging competitively priced shipments (*lpi_price*)
- the efficiency of customs clearance processes (i.e. speed, simplicity and predictability of formalities) (*lpi_customs*)
- the quality of trade and transport-related infrastructure (e.g. ports, railroads, roads, information technology) (*lpi_infra*)
- how often the shipments to the assessed country reach the consignee within the scheduled or expected delivery time (*lpi_freq*).

Scores are averaged across all respondents and all indices range from 1 to 5: the higher the score the better the performance.

Figure 2.16 plots the share of counterfeit and pirated goods exported by each economy against their LPI scores in 2013. It is interesting to note that economies that combine relatively (i) more competitive priced shipments; (ii) fast and simple customs clearance processes; and (ii) high-quality transport infrastructure seem to export more counterfeit and pirated products than others. On the other hand, the greater an economy's ability to track and trace consignments, the lower its share of fake exports. Finally, the nature of the relationship is unclear between an economy's competence and the quality of its logistics services and the reliability of its scheduled or expected delivery time. The results of the fractional response model related to LPIs presented below will shed further light on these relationships.

2.4.2. Results

The results of the fractional response model highlight some important insights into the impact of logistics facilities on the magnitude of counterfeit and pirated trade.

First, **the ability to trace and track consignments is a key factor in reducing the share of counterfeit and pirated products exported by an economy** (see Table A.1, Annex A). This is indicated by the negative sign associated with the respective component of logistic performance index in Table A.1, and the magnitude of this impact, which is larger than for the other logistics indicators (Figure 2.17).

The left-hand graph in Figure 2.17 indicates that the share of counterfeit and pirated exports in total exports for economies that cannot easily trace and track consignments is on average 7.5%, compared with only 0.5% for economies that have perfected this ability. In addition, the right-hand graph in Figure 2.17 suggests that **enhancing the ability to trace and track shipments would reduce the share of counterfeit and pirated products exported by economies that are currently highly corrupt.**

Figure 2.16. Relationship between the share of exports of fakes and the Logistics Performance Index, 2013

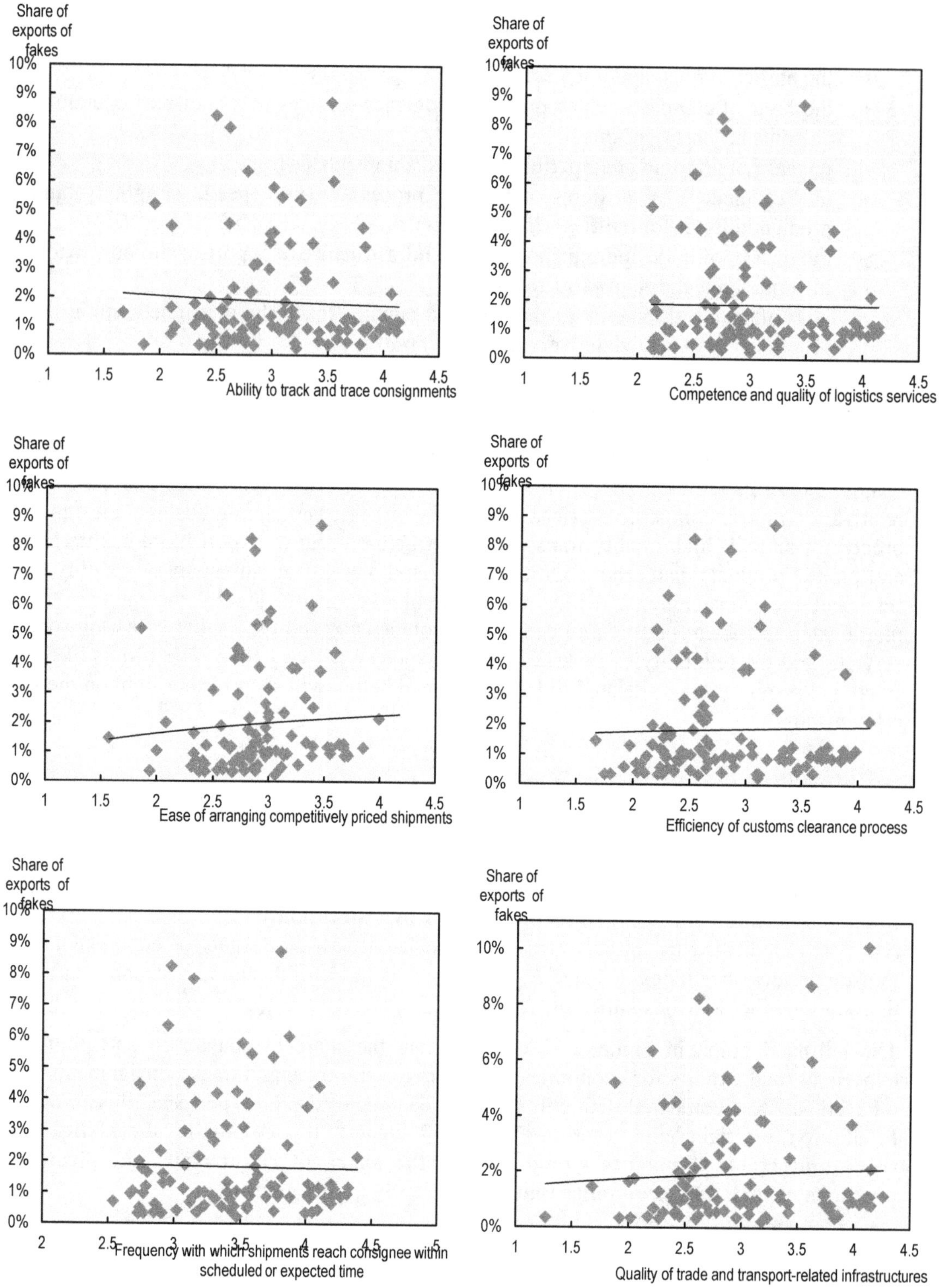

Notes: Each point corresponds to one economy. Logistics performance scores lie between 1 and 5, with higher scores corresponding to better outcomes.

Source: Authors' own calculations based on OECD/EUIPO (2016)[1] and World Bank and Turku School of Economics (2018)[13].

Figure 2.17. Impact of the ability to trace and track consignments on the share of counterfeit and pirated exports

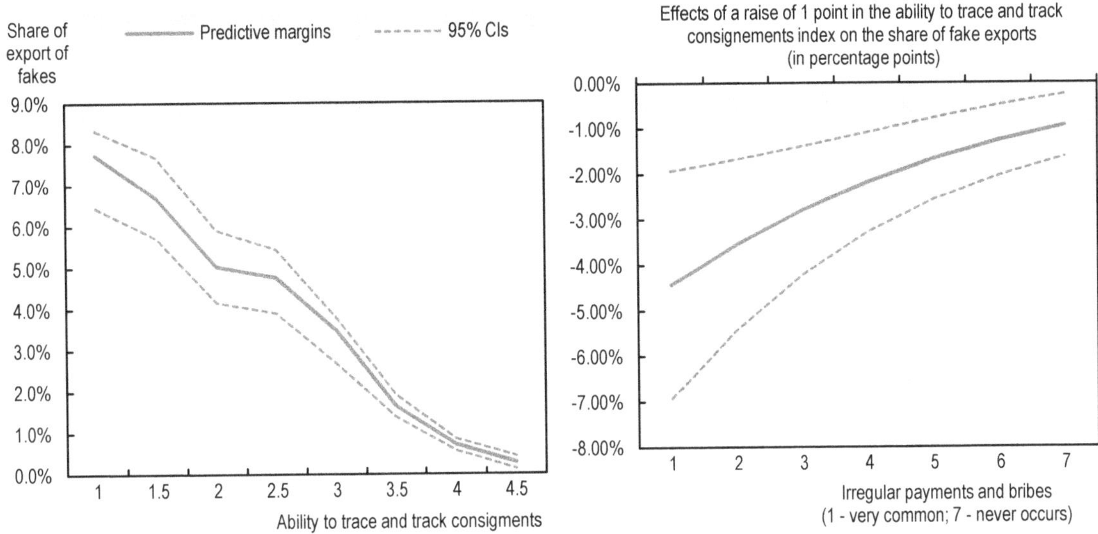

Notes: Calculations based on model 1 of Table A.1, Annex A. "CIs" stand for "confidence intervals". The left-hand graph indicates the average share of counterfeit and pirated exports for economies depending on the score for their ability to trace and track consignments (see the description of the logistics indicators in section 2.4.1). The right-hand side of the figure indicates the effect of a reduction of 1 point of this score on the conditional mean of an economy's share of counterfeit and pirated exports depending on the index for irregular payments and bribes. The index of irregular payments and bribes was built on the following question: "how common is it for firms to make undocumented extra payments or bribes connected with (a) imports and exports; (b) public utilities; (c) annual tax payments; (d) awarding of public contracts and licenses; (e) obtaining favorable judicial decisions?", where 1 = very common; 7 = never occurs.

Another important insight is that in economies where (i) **it is easy to arrange competitively priced shipments**; (ii) **customs clearance processes are efficient**; and (iii) **trade and transport-related infrastructure** (e.g. ports, railroads, roads, information technology) is high quality, **the share of counterfeit and pirated products exported significantly increases** (Table A.1, Annex A).

However, and this is particularly important concerning customs clearance processes, **these relationships are especially true for economies with weak governance**. This is illustrated in Figure 2.18, which shows for instance that a raise of one point for the ease of arranging competitive priced shipments or in the speed and simplicity of customs formalities increases on average the share of counterfeit and pirated exports by 3 percentage points for economies where irregular payments and bribes are very common. Yet they would have almost no effect on the share of fake exports for economies where irregular payments and bribes never occur.

Finally, according to Table A.1, the two remaining logistics facilities – the frequency with which shipments reach consignees within the scheduled or expected time, and the level of competence and quality of logistics services (e.g. transport operators, customs brokers) – appear to have no significant impact on the share of counterfeit and pirated exports.

Figure 2.18. Impact on fake exports of improving trade and customs-related infrastructure in a context of corruption

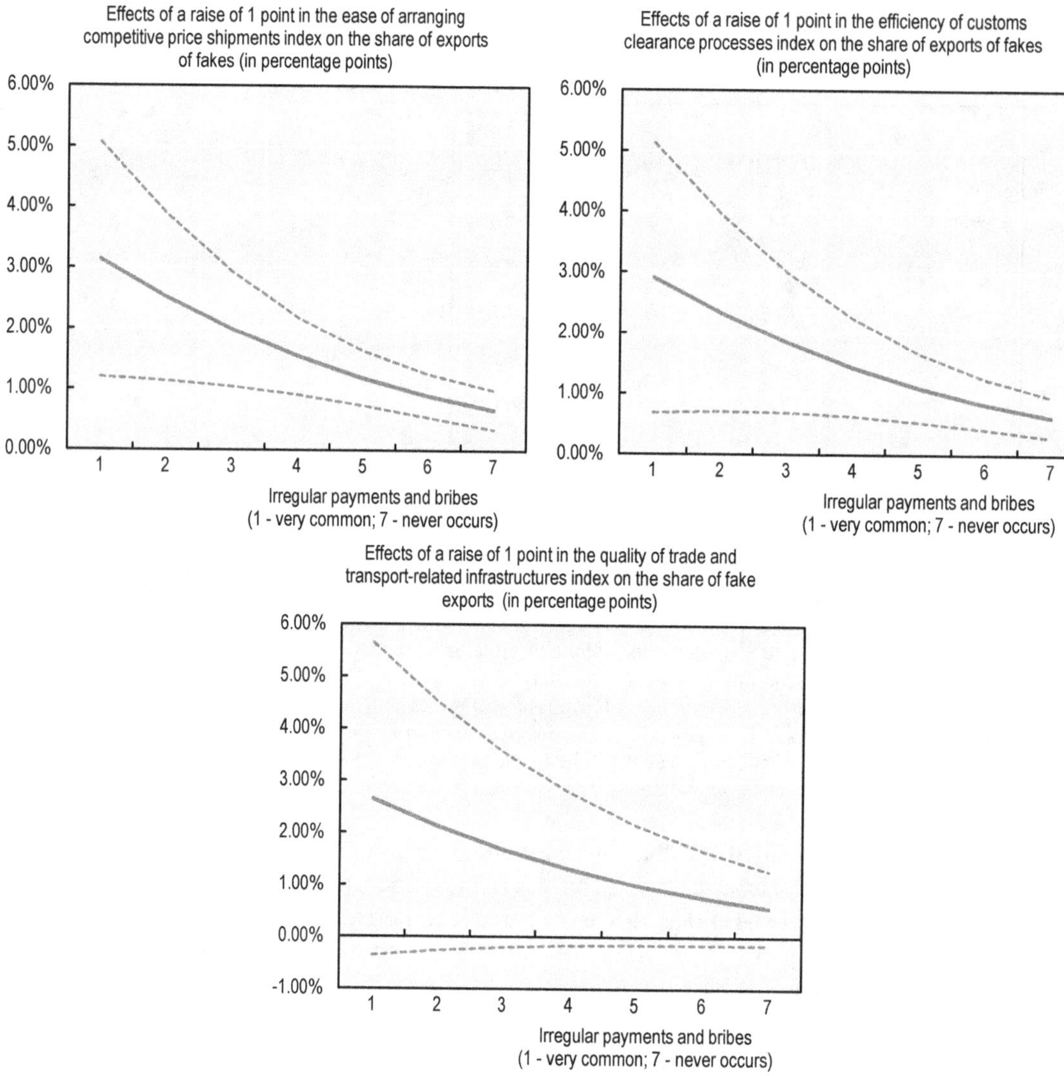

Notes: Calculations based on model 1 of Table A.1, Annex A. Average marginal effects on the conditional mean. Description of logisitics performance score is presented in Section 2.4.1. "CIs" stand for "confidence intervals". The index of irregular payments and bribes was built on the following question: "how common is it for firms to make undocumented extra payments or bribes connected with (a) imports and exports; (b) public utilities; (c) annual tax payments; (d) awarding of public contracts and licenses; (e) obtaining favorable judicial decisions?", where 1 = very common; 7 = never occurs.

2.5. Trade facilitation index

The gains from making the process of trade easier are real and obvious (OECD, 2005[14]). Governments gain because efficient border procedures allow them to process more goods and improve fraud control, thus increasing government revenue. Businesses gain because if they can deliver goods more quickly to their customers they are more competitive. And consumers gain because they are not paying the costs of lengthy border delays.

On the one hand, a large number of specific trade facilitation measures clearly help both the ease of doing business and the fight against counterfeit trade and smuggling. On the other hand, some trade facilitations measures might help counterfeiters and pirates to integrate more easily into global supply chains. This would be the case, for instance, if the simplification of documents or streamlining of border procedures are not accompanied by sufficient staff training or the recruitment of new staff competent in checking for fraud.

2.5.1. Description of data

This study uses the OECD Trade Facilitation Indicators (TFIs) (OECD, 2018[15]) to investigate if and how trade facilitation measures affect the share of counterfeit and pirated products exported by economies. OECD TFIs were created to provide a tool for countries to visualise the state of implementation of the various policy areas and measures included under the World Trade Organization (WTO) (OECD, 2015[16]). They cover the full spectrum of border procedures, from advance rulings to transit guarantees, as follows:

- Information availability (tfi_a), e.g. publication of trade information, including on the Internet; transparency of required documentation; user manuals; available legislation; enquiry points.
- Involvement of trade community (tfi_b), i.e. structure for consultations with traders; established guidelines for consultations; publications of drafts; existence of notice-and-comment frameworks.
- Advance rulings (tfi_c), i.e. prior statements by the administration to requesting traders concerning the classification, origin, valuation method, etc., applied to specific goods at the time of importation; the rules and process applied to such statements.
- Appeal procedures (tfi_d), i.e. the possibility and modalities available to appeal administrative decisions by border agencies.
- Fees and charges (tfi_e), i.e. disciplines on the fees and charges imposed on imports and exports; transparency and regular review of fees and charges; disciplines on transparency and implementation of penalties systems.
- Formalities – documents (tfi_f), i.e. acceptance of copies, simplification of trade documents; harmonisation in accordance with international standards.
- Formalities – automation (tfi_g), i.e. electronic exchange of data; use of automated risk management; automated border procedures; electronic payments; automated pre-arrival processing; digital signatures.
- Formalities – procedures (tfi_h), i.e. streamlining of border controls; single submission points for all required documentation (single windows); post-clearance audits; authorised operators; measures on perishable goods; risk management systems; expedited shipments.
- Border agency co-operation – internal (tfi_i), i.e. control delegation to customs authorities; co-operation between various border agencies of the country.
- Border agency co-operation – external (tfi_j), i.e. co-operation with neighbouring and third countries.

All these trade facilitation indicators for 2013 are plotted against the share of counterfeit and pirated exports estimates by OECD/EUIPO (2016)[1] in Figure 2.19.

Figure 2.19. Relationship between the share of exports of fakes and the Trade Facilitation Indicators, 2013

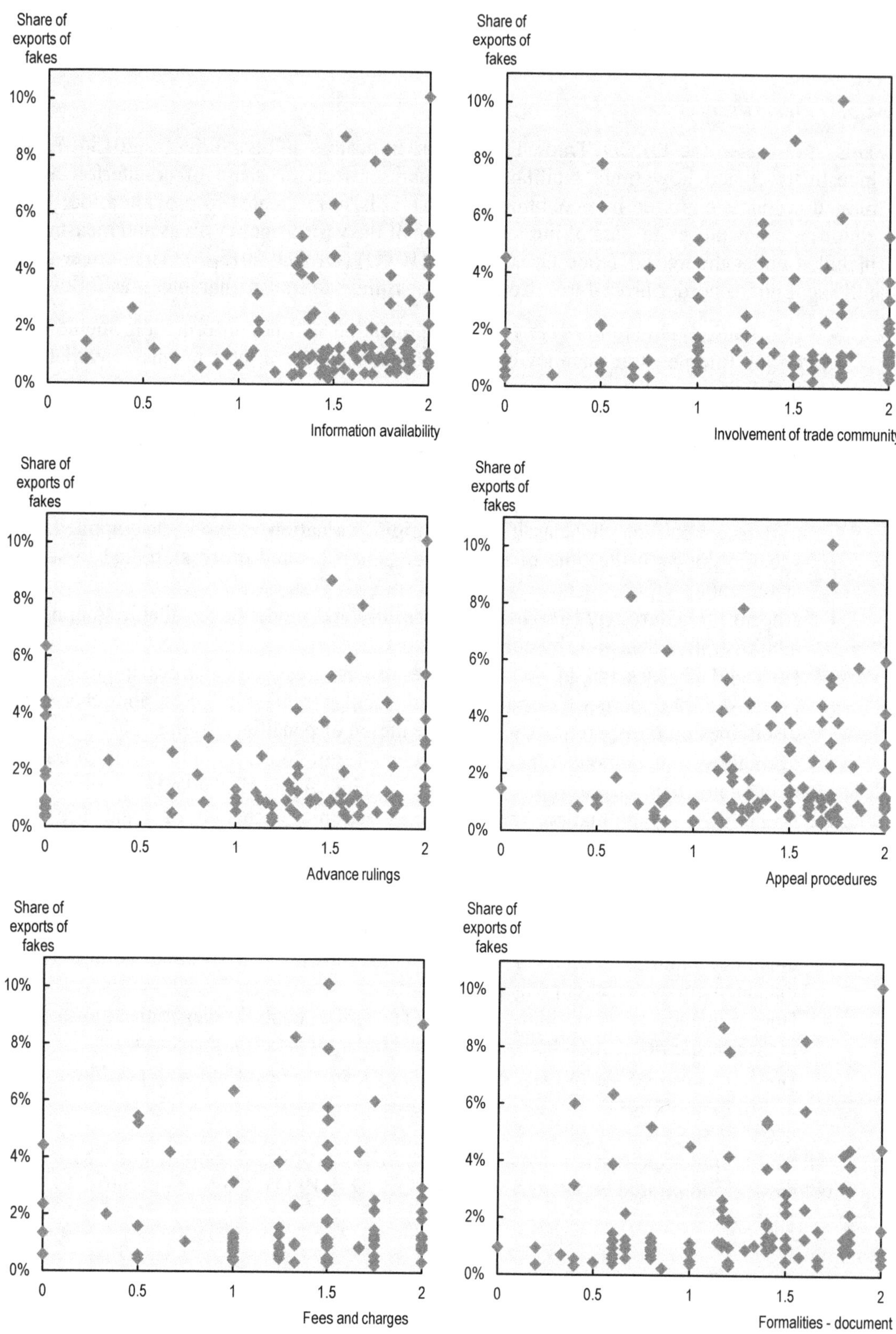

Figure 2.19. Relationship between the share of exports of fakes and the Trade Facilitation Indicators, 2013 (*continued*)

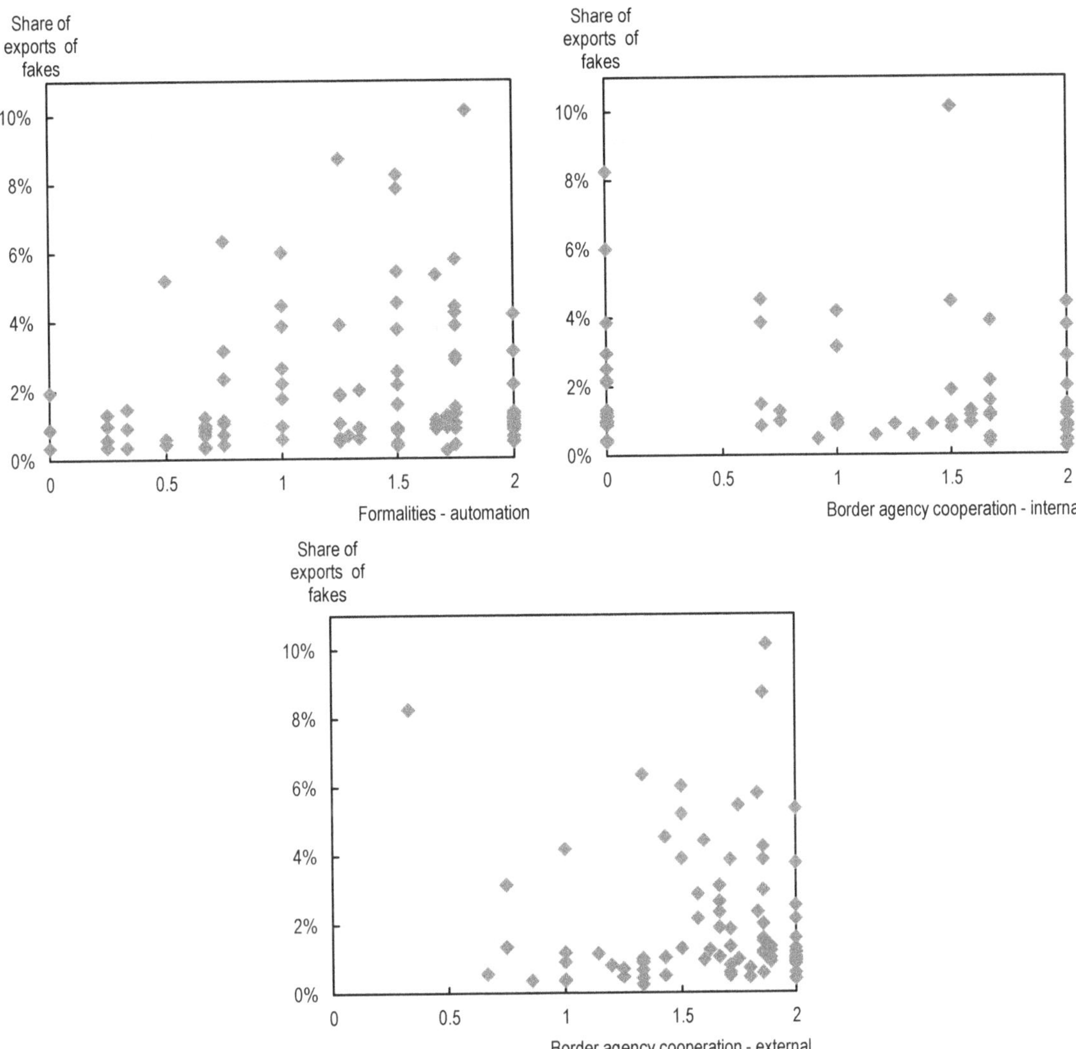

Notes: Each point corresponds to one economy. Trade Facilitation Indicators range from 1 to 2, with higher scores corresponding to better outcomes.
Source: Authors' own calculations based on OECD/EUIPO (2016)[1] and OECD (2018)[15].

2.5.2. Results

One of the most important insights in Table A.1 (Annex A) and Figure 2.19 is that the following **four trade policies and measures seemingly can help an economy to reduce the share of counterfeit and pirated products in its exports**:

1. **Greater availability of trade information** (e.g. publication of trade information, including on the Internet; transparency of required documentation; user manuals; available legislation; enquiry points).
2. **Deeper involvement in the world trade community** (i.e. structure for consultations with traders; established guidelines for consultations; publications of drafts; existence of notice-and-comment frameworks).

3. **More disciplined, transparent and regularly reviewed fees and charges imposed on imports and exports**; and disciplines on transparency and implementation of penalties systems; and
4. **Better border agency internal co-operation** (i.e. control delegation to customs authorities; co-operation between various border agencies of the country).

The magnitudes of these impacts are presented in the first four figures of Figure 2.20, which indicates for instance that the share of counterfeit and pirated exports is on average 2.6% for economies where the availability and transparency of trade information is poor (a score of 0 on the TFI index), compared to 1.1% for economies where this information is perfectly transparent and available (a score of 2 on the TFI index).

On the other hand, the results in Table A.1 (Annex A) indicate that **counterfeit and pirated trade tends to be encouraged by trade policies and measures concerning** (i) **advance rulings** (i.e. prior statements by the administration to requesting traders concerning the classification, origin, valuation method, etc., applied to specific goods at the time of importation; as well as the rules and process applied to such statements); and (ii) the **possibility and modalities to appeal administrative decisions by border agencies**.

This is illustrated by the last two graphs in Figure 2.20, which show that the average share of fake exports for economies with many options and ways of appealing administrative decisions by border agencies (a score of 2 on the TFI index) is 1.3%, compared with 1.8% for economies where these options do not exist (a score of 0 on the TFI index).

Finally, trade policies and measures concerning formalities (documents, automation and procedures) appear to have no influence on the magnitude of counterfeit and pirated trade. However, note that this could be related to the fact that the logistic performance index measuring the "efficiency" of customs clearance processes (i.e the speed, simplicity and predictability of customs formalities) already captures this impact (see Section 2.4).

A final important result concerning counterfeit and pirated trade and trade facilitation policies is that **the impact of trade facilitation measures on the share of exports of fakes largely depends on the level of corruption**.

This is shown in Figure 2.21 below, which reveals that improvements in trade policies and measures concerning trade information availability, disciplines on fees and charges, internal border agency co-operation, and the involvement in the trade community in particular would reduce the share of counterfeit and pirated products exported by economies that are currently highly corrupt. For instance, a raise of 1 point in the internal border agency co-operation score would reduce the share of fake exports on average by 1.5 percentage points for economies where irregular payments and bribes are very common, compared with only 0.33 percentage points for economies where bribery never occurs.

Figure 2.20. Predicted impact of various trade facilitation policies on exports of fakes

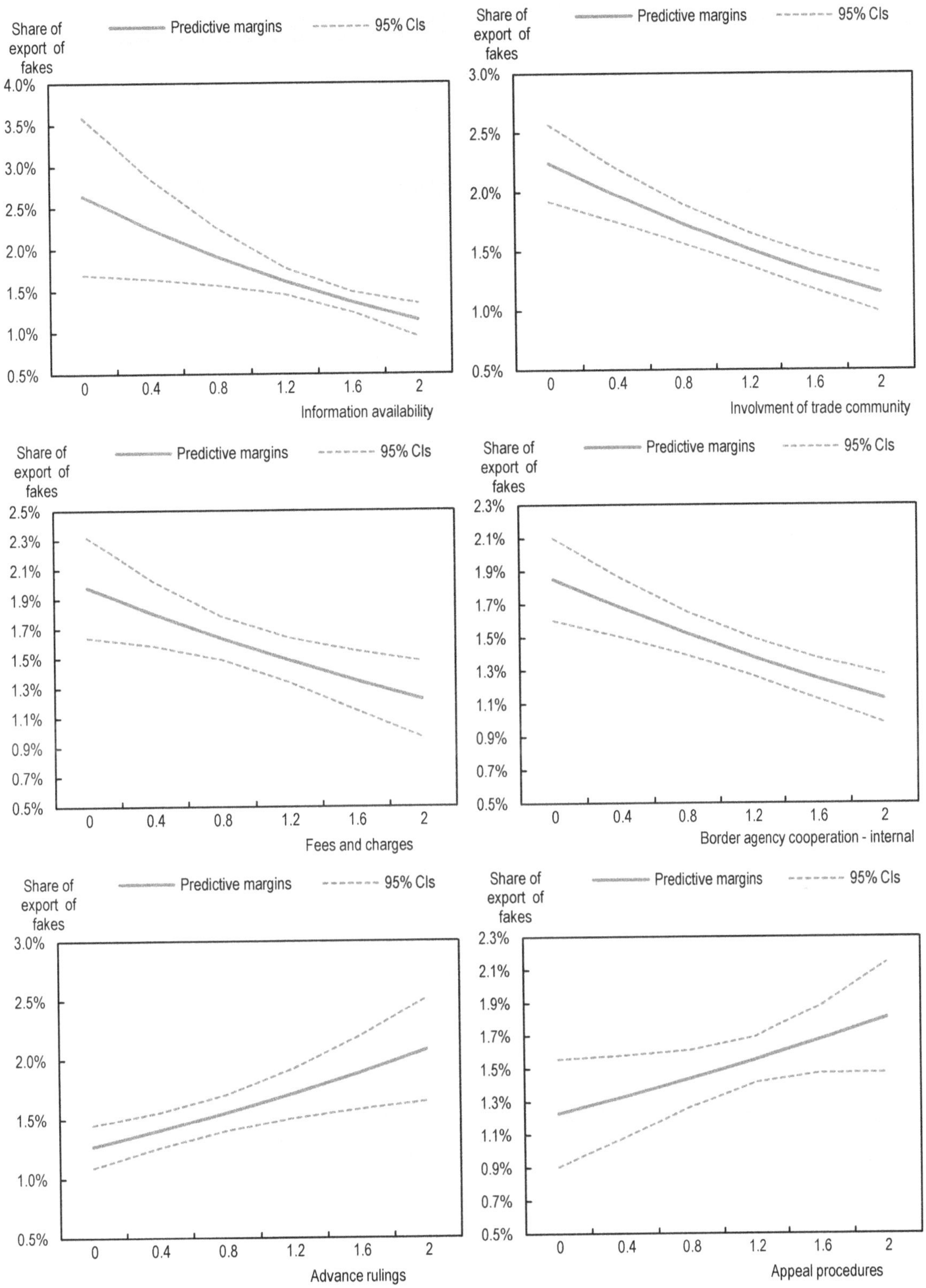

Notes: Calculations are based on model 1 displayed in Table A.1. "CIs" stands for "confidence intervals". A description of trade facilitation indices are presented in Section 2.5.1.

Figure 2.21. Impact of improving trade facilitation measures on the share of exports of fakes in economies where irregular payments and bribes are common

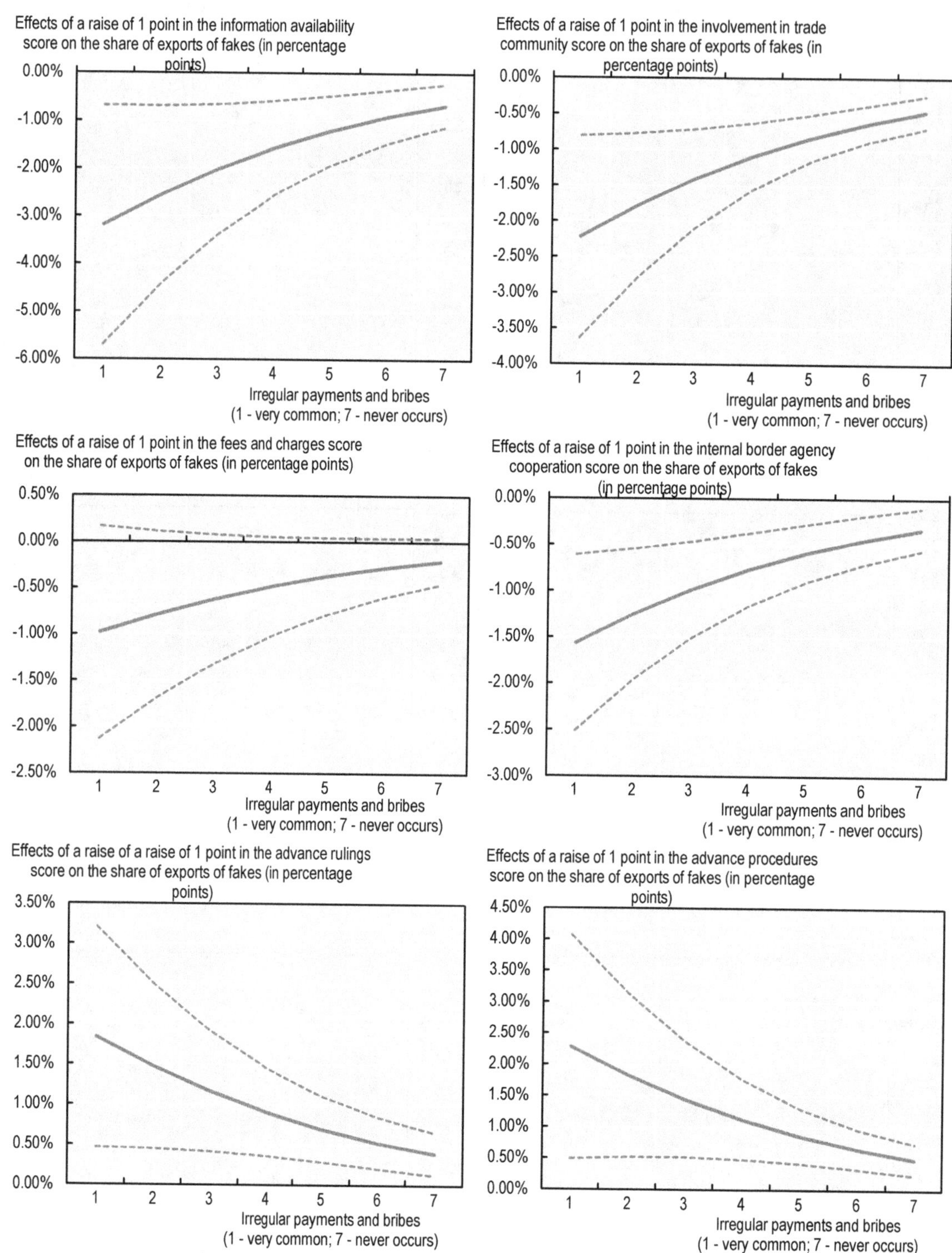

Note: Calculations based on model 1 of Table A.1, Annex A. "CIs" stand for "confidence intervals". Average marginal effects on the conditional mean. Description of trade facilitation indices are presented in Section 2.5.1. The index of irregular payments and bribes was built on the following question: "how common is it for firms to make undocumented extra payments or bribes connected with (a) imports and exports; (b) public utilities; (c) annual tax payments; (d) awarding of public contracts and licenses; (e) obtaining favorable judicial decisions?", where 1 = very common; 7 = never occurs.

References

Arvis, J. et al. (2016), *Connecting to Compete 2016: Trade Logistics in the Global Economy*, World Bank, Washington, DC.

Kaufmann, D., A. Kraay and M. Mastruzzi (2010), *The Worldwide Governance Indicators: Methodology and Analytical Issues*, World Bank Policy Research Working Paper No. 5430, World Bank, Washington, DC, http://papers.ssrn.com/sol3/papers.cfm?abstract_id=1682130.

Long, J. (1997), "Regression Models for Categorical and Limited Dependent Variables", *Sage Publishing*.

OECD (2018), *Trade Facilitation Indicators*, http://www.oecd.org/trade/facilitation/indicators.htm.

OECD (2017), *Customs Integrity: Taking Stock of Good Practices*, http://www.oecd.org/gov/ethics/G20-integrity-in-customs-taking-stock-of-good-practices.pdf.

OECD (2015), *OECD Trade Facilitation Indicators: An overview of available tools:*, http://www.oecd.org/tad/facilitation/TFIs-overview-available-tools-september-2015.pdf.

OECD (2008), *The Economic Impact of Counterfeiting and Piracy*, OECD Publishing, Paris, http:// www.oecd.org/sti/ind/theeconomicimpactofcounterfeitingandpiracy.htm.

OECD (2005), *The Costs and Benefits of Trade Facilitation*, OECD Policy Brief, http://www.oecd.org/trade/facilitation/35459690.pdf.

OECD/EUIPO (2018), *Trade in Counterfeit Goods and Free Trade Zones: Evidence from Recent Trends*, OECD Publishing, Paris/EUIPO, http://dx.doi.org/10.1787/9789264289550-en.

OECD/EUIPO (2016), *Trade in Counterfeit and Pirated Goods: Mapping the Economic Impact*, OECD Publishing, Paris, http://dx.doi.org/10.1787/9789264252653-en.

Papke, L. and J. Wooldridge (1996), "Econometric methods for fractional response variables with an application to 401(K) plan participation rates", *Journal of Applied Econometrics*, Vol. 11/6, pp. 619-632.

Schwab, K. and X. Sala-i-Martin (2015), *The Global Competetiveness Report 2014-2015*, World Economic Forum.

World Bank (2014), *Doing Business Data*, World Bank, Washington, DC, http://www.doingbusiness.org/data.

World Bank and Turku School of Economics (2018), *Logistic Performance Index Surveys*, World Bank, Washington, DC, http://www.worldbank.org/lpi.

Yücer, A., J. Siroën and E. Archanskaia (2014), *World FTZ Database*, http://ftz.dauphine.fr (accessed on November 2017).

Notes

[1] See OECD/EUIPO (2018)[9] for a complete description of the data.

[2] In the source database the term export processing zones (EPZs) is used.

3. Conclusions and next steps

This chapter presents an overview of the findings from the analysis. It summarises the key, economy-specific factors that appear to drive trade in counterfeit and pirated goods and lists steps that could be taken to enhance future work.

This study has quantitatively examined the observable socio-economic factors that may explain why some economies emerge as important producers of fake goods, or as transit points in their global trade. This question is motivated by the OECD-EUIPO (2016)[1] study, which found that virtually any economy in the world can be a provenance of counterfeit and pirated trade, either as a place that produces infringing goods or as a point of transit through which infringing goods pass.

The OECD-EUIPO (2016)[1] study identified 173 provenance economies of counterfeit and pirated products. The study also noted that some of these provenance economies are more important sources of infringing goods than others. This could be because they are important producers of IP infringing goods or because they are strategic points of transit. In addition, some provenance economies can specialise in a certain types of goods, in certain modes of transport, etc.

3.1. What have we learnt?

3.1.1. The key factors

This report provides more detailed and precise information about the quantifiable socio-economic conditions that appear to drive economies' propensities to become active actors in the trade in fake goods. It complements the available data on trade in counterfeit and pirated goods with a wealth of country-level statistics that illustrate economies' social, economic and political levels of development, and makes the link between these and their level of counterfeit trade activities. Table 3.1 summarises the effects of the indicators chosen on the likelihood of an economy to engage in counterfeit production or trade.

Table 3.1. What factors influence the trade in fake goods?

Category	Factor	Effect on trade in fakes
Production facilities	Minimum wage	Reduces
	Annual paid leave	Reduces
Free trade zones	Number of FTZs in an economy	Enhances
Governance indicators*	Irregular payments and bribes (WEF)	Enhances
	Intellectual property protection (WEF)	Reduces
	Control of corruption (World Bank)	Reduces
Trade facilitation	Information ability	Reduces
	Involvement of trade community	Reduces
	Advance rulings	Enhances
	Appeal procedures	Enhances
	Fees and charges	Reduces
	Border agency internal cooperation	Reduces
Logistics performance	Ability to track and trace consignments	Reduces
	Competitive priced shipments	Enhances
	Efficiency of customs clearance process	Enhances
	Quality of transport infrastructure	Enhances

Note: *Governance indicators have been found to be an additional catalysis of the effects of other factors on the trade in fakes – see the discussion below.

For the first category – production facilities – economies with the lowest labour costs and the poorest working conditions have the largest share of counterfeit and pirated exports. The analysis suggests that an improvement of working conditions, i.e raising the minimum wage or increasing the number of days of paid leave, would decrease the share of counterfeit and pirated products exported by economies, especially those whose governance is weak.

In terms of governance, the results highlight that the level of corruption and the quality of intellectual property protection are important drivers of counterfeit and pirated trade. The share of fakes in exports is significantly larger for economies where irregular payments and bribes are very common, or where the control of corruption is very poor. On the other hand, the share of counterfeit and pirated exports is significantly lower for economies where intellectual property protection is very strong.

The presence of free trade zones seems to be a strong factor in encouraging trade in counterfeits. The results indicate that on average, the share of counterfeit and pirated products in exports from economies without FTZs is 50% lower than for economies hosting many FTZs.

The impact of logistics facilities on the magnitude of counterfeit and pirated trade is more nuanced, and depends on the corruption levels in a given economy. On the one hand the ability to trace and track consignments is a key factor in reducing the share of counterfeit and pirated products exported. Thus, increasing the ability to trace and track shipments could significantly reduce the share of counterfeit and pirated products exported by economies that are currently highly corrupt. On the other hand, other logistics factors are associated with an increased counterfeit trade, including low shipping prices; speedy, simple and predictable customs formalities; and good quality trade and transport infrastructure (e.g. ports, railroads, roads and information technology). However, these relationships are particularly strong for economies whose governance is weak.

Similar conclusions can be drawn for the trade facilitation indices. Four features are associated with a low level of counterfeit and pirated exports: easily available trade information; a deep involvement in the world trade community; transparent and regularly reviewed fees and charges imposed on imports and exports; and sound co-operation between border agency and other government units. Importantly, however, the overall impact of these factors largely depends on the level of corruption. The analysis finds that the higher the level of corruption in an economy, the greater the effects of trade facilitation on increasing trade in fakes.

Importantly, governance is a crucial element in either enhancing or reducing the intensity of trade in fakes. Governance factors, in addition to their direct effect, also multiply the influence of other elements (FTZs, quality of logistic facilities or trade facilitation policies) on the share of counterfeits in exports. Therefore, good governance could greatly deter the effects of logistics, trade measures or FTZs on illicit trade in counterfeits.

There are three important general comments to note in this context:

First, none of the factors outlined above *alone* explain the phenomenon of exports of fakes from an economy. It is the combination of these factors that allows important nodes in trade in counterfeit and pirated goods to emerge.

Second, many of the factors that contribute to counterfeit trade are also very beneficial for general trade flows. For example, good logistics facilities are desirable from the trade perspective in terms of efficiency and their welfare-enhancing effect. It is the *misuse* of these facilities, usually in the context of corruption and other governance-related failures, that is the problem.

Finally, improving governance and institutional quality matters for reducing the volume of counterfeit exports from manufacturing countries. It seems however that it has less impact on reducing the volume of counterfeits that pass through transit countries. Incentives to stop counterfeits going through transit countries are generally low as there is a relatively low risk that counterfeits shipped through these countries will end up within their borders and services related to the transit of goods may be important source of revenue for local firms. As a result, even countries with high governance standards and high institutional quality may have no interest in reducing the volume of counterfeit trade.

3.1.2. Targeting policies to regional profiles

The analysis presented above has identified a set of factors related to the intensity of export of counterfeit and pirated products from an economy. A closer look at the profiles of selected major provenance economies of counterfeit and pirated products identified in the existing OECD/EUIPO studies leads to two interesting findings:

1. Some important provenance economies identified by OECD/EUIPO (2017)[2] have very advanced socio-economic profiles. For example, Hong Kong (China) and Singapore are characterised by high levels of GDP per capita, and high governance quality. Trade plays a very important role for these economies: they score very highly for their share of trade in GDP, as well as for the quality and performance of logistics infrastructure and trade facilitation measures. Yet together, these two economies are associated with 20% of all seizures in the OECD/EUIPO dataset of customs seizures (19.5% for Hong Kong and 0.5% for Singapore) (OECD/EUIPO, 2016[1]).[1]

2. There are also several important provenance economies, such as Senegal, Pakistan and Ghana, that are generally among the poorest performers in terms of governance quality, and have low scores for the importance of trade in their GDP. Their levels of GDP per capita, and trade facilitation and logistics infrastructure, are generally low.[2]

Information such as this can help in developing targeted and effective policies for countering counterfeit trade, is discussed below.

3.2. Next steps

The quantitative analysis presented here has identified several research areas that might merit further investigation. A more in-depth analysis of these topics could be beneficial for developing efficient enforcement and governance frameworks to counter the substantial risks posed by trade in counterfeit goods:

- Good governance is essential for effective action against illicit trade in counterfeits. Poor governance, corruption and weak IPR enforcement enable counterfeiters to misuse logistics and trade facilities. Further investigation into how good governance and sound IPR enforcement can prevent trade in counterfeit goods is needed – either at the industry level or through a case-by-case analysis. This investigation could take into account more nuanced aspects of the dynamic between corruption, poor governance and insufficient IPR enforcement and the trade in fakes, such as the impact of corruption at various levels of governance on the incentive context for customs and enforcement agencies.

- Some important provenance economies are characterised by seemingly sound governance and good quality infrastructure. It could be useful for policymakers to probe more deeply into why these economies are such important nodes for the trade in fake goods in order to tailor policies accordingly. A judiciously chosen hybrid of gravity variables and fixed and random effects could be used, which would have the advantage of avoiding a logistics function approach and would reflect the trade nature of the data.

- Some provenance economies have low income levels, weak governance and poor infrastructure. The potential for combatting illicit trade in these economies is likely to be particularly high, and the marginal returns from improving governance structures to counter illicit trade could be particularly beneficial. Further investigation could provide more information about the nature of counterfeit trade in these economies, and help to identify "low hanging fruit" in terms of policy solutions to counter this threat.

References

Kaufmann, D., A. Kraay and M. Mastruzzi (2010), *The Worldwide Governance Indicators: Methodology and Analytical Issues*, World Bank Policy Research Working Paper No. 5430, World Bank, Washington, DC, http://papers.ssrn.com/sol3/papers.cfm?abstract_id=1682130.

OECD (2018), *Trade Facilitation Indicators*, http://www.oecd.org/trade/facilitation/indicators.htm.

OECD/EUIPO (2017), *Mapping the Real Routes of Trade in Fake Goods*, OECD Publishing, Paris, http://dx.doi.org/10.1787/9789264278349-en.

OECD/EUIPO (2016), *Trade in Counterfeit and Pirated Goods: Mapping the Economic Impact*, OECD Publishing, Paris, http://dx.doi.org/10.1787/9789264252653-en.

Schwab, K. and X. Sala-i-Martin (2015), *The Global Competetiveness Report 2014-2015*, World Economic Forum.

World Bank (2014), *Doing Business Data*, World Bank, Washington, DC, http://www.doingbusiness.org/data.

World Bank and Turku School of Economics (2018), *Logistic Performance Index Surveys*, World Bank, Washington, DC, http://www.worldbank.org/lpi.

Notes

[1] Hong Kong (China) is number 1 and Singapore number 33 in the GTRIC-e score list of countries for their propensity to export fakes (OECD/EUIPO, 2016). In percentage terms (in relation to the average for all analysed countries), the relevant measures for Hong Kong (China) (HKG) and Singapore (SGP) are: GDP per capita: 132% (HKG), 236% (SGP); Control of corruption 60% (HKG), 77% (SGP); IPR Protection 59% (HKG), 59% (SGP); Share of trade in GDP :574% (HKG), 375% (SGP); Border agency internal co-operation: 34% (HKG), 60% (SGP); Ability to track and trace shipments: 38% (HKG), 37% (SGP)

[2] Pakistan is number 19, and Senegal is number 21 in the GTRIC-e score list for their propensity to export fakes (OECD/EUIPO, 2016). In percentage terms (in relation to the average for all analysed countries), the relevant measures for Pakistan (PAK) and Senegal (SEN) are: GDP per capita: -92% (PAK), -94% (SEN); Control of corruption -41% (PAK), -11% (SEN); IPR Protection -25% (PAK), -7% (SEN); Share of trade in GDP :-62% (PAK), -38% (SEN); Border agency internal co-operation: 20% (PAK), -20% (SEN); Ability to track and trace shipments: -13% (PAK), -29% (SEN)

Annex A. Additional tables

Table A A.1. Determinants of the share of counterfeit and pirated exports, 2011-2013

Fractional response model[1]

	(1)	(2)	(3)	(4)
Share of the manufacturing sector in value added	1.111	0.999	1.191	1.761
	(0.762)[2]	(0.778)	(0.770)	(0.785)
Minimum wage (in log)	-0.032***[3]	-0.031***	-0.034***	-0.027***
	(0.009)	(0.009)	(0.009)	(0.010)
Annual paid leave	-0.015***	-0.014***	-0.014***	-0.015***
	(0.001)	(0.004)	(0.004)	(0.004)
Number of FTZs	0.009*	0.011***	0.010***	0.011***
	(0.004)	(0.003)	(0.004)	(0.004)
Irregular payments and bribes (WEF)	-0.126***		-0.082*	
	(0.035)		(0.044)	
Intellectual property protection (WEF)		-0.154***	-0.110**	
		(0.042)	(0.054)	
Control of corruption (World Bank)				-0.086**
				(0.042)
Trade facilitation: Information ability	-0.372***	-0.388***	-0.415***	-0.337***
	(0.108)	(0.107)	(0.107)	(0.113)
Trade facilitation: Involvement of trade community	-0.259***	-0.260***	-0.276***	-0.282***
	(0.049)	(0.048)	(0.048)	(0.048)
Trade facilitation: Advance rulings	0.214***	0.197***	0.200***	0.231***
	(0.064)	(0.062)	(0.064)	(0.063)
Trade facilitation: Appeal procedures	0.266***	0.291***	0.317***	0.179**
	(0.067)	(0.074)	(0.074)	(0.077)
Trade facilitation: Fees and charges	-0.114*	-0.130*	-0.098	-0.213***
	(0.066)	(0.075)	(0.068)	(0.070)
Trade facilitation: Formalities - documents	0.078	0.078	0.078	0.089
	(0.064)	(0.057)	(0.059)	(0.065)
Trade facilitation: Formalities - automation	-0.003	0.003	0.021	-0.074
	(0.066)	(0.063)	(0.064)	(0.063)
Trade facilitation: Formalities - procedures	0.061	0.026	0.041	0.096
	(0.108)	(0.104)	(0.102)	(0.119)
Trade facilitation: Border agency internal cooperation	-0.182***	-0.134***	-0.136***	-0.216***
	(0.046)	(0.043)	(0.045)	(0.046)
Trade facilitation: Border agency external cooperation	0.011	-0.015	-0.005	0.032
	(0.030)	(0.031)	(0.031)	(0.029)
Logistics performance index: Ability to track and trace consignments	-0.516***	-0.412***	-0.421***	-0.647***
	(0.135)	(0.142)	(0.133)	(0.144)
Logistics performance index: Competence and quality of logistics services	-0.356	-0.230	-0.277	-0.279
	(0.298)	(0.231)	(0.221)	(0.223)
Logistics performance index: Competitive priced shipments	0.731***	0.613***	0.651***	0.859***
	(0.137)	(0.133)	(0.139)	(0.131)

	(1)	(2)	(3)	(4)
Logistics performance index: Efficiency of customs clearance process	0.678***	0.565***	0.709***	0.626***
	(0.171)	(0.168)	(0.170)	(0.180)
Logistics performance index: Frequency with which shipments reach consignee within scheduled or expected time	-0.140	-0.182	-0.109	-0.154
	(0.118)	(0.114)	(0.115)	(0.121)
Logistics performance index: Quality of transport infrastructure	0.308*	0.386**	0.337*	0.324*
	(0.177)	(0.174)	(0.177)	(0.187)
_cons	-0.893***	-1.233***	-1.178***	-0.769**
	(0.295)	(0.284)	(0.290)	(0.313)
Pseudo R-squared4	0.026***	0.026***	0.027***	0.044***
Number of observations	176	176	176	179
Chi2	259.568	291.594	289.083	521.516

Note: 1) For a description of the fractional response model, see Box 2.1 in Section 2. 2) Robust standard errors in parenthesis. 3) *p<0.05; **p<0.01; ***p<0.001.4) The model estimates from the fractional logistic regression are maximum likelihood estimates arrived at through an iterative process. They are not calculated to minimize variance, so the OLS approach to interpret the R-squared does not apply. Pseudo R-squared values displayed in this table are McFadden's pseudo R-squared, which mirrors the adjusted R-squared in OLS by penalizing a model for including too many predictors. If the predictors in the model are effective, then the penalty will be small relative to the added information of the predictors. However, if a model contains predictors that do not add sufficiently to the model, then the penalty becomes noticeable and the adjusted R-squared can decrease with the addition of a predictor, even if the R-squared increases slightly. Note that negative McFadden's adjusted R-squared are possible. They thus cannot be interpreted as one would interpret an OLS R-squared and different pseudo R-squared can arrive at very different values.

Table A A.2. Description of variables

Variable	Variable description	Source	Source description
		Variable to be explained	
Share of fake exports	Share of the value of counterfeit and pirated exports into total exports by provenance economy and year over the period 2011-2013	OECD/EUIPO (2016)[1]	
		Explanatory variables	
		Governance indicators	
Control of corruption	"Control of Corruption" measures perceptions of corruption, conventionally defined as the exercise of public power for private gain. The particular aspect of corruption measured by the various sources differs somewhat, ranging from the frequency of "additional payments to get things done", to the effects of corruption on the business environment, to measuring "grand corruption" in the political arena or in the tendency of elite forms to engage in "state capture".	World Bank Governance Indicators (Kaufmann, Kraay and Mastruzzi, 2010[7])	The Worldwide Governance Indicators are based on several hundred individual variables measuring perceptions of governance, drawn from 31 separate data sources constructed by 25 different organizations. The governance estimates are normally distributed with a mean of zero and a standard deviation of one each year of measurement. This implies that virtually all scores lie between -2.5 and 2.5, with higher scores corresponding to better outcomes.
Irregular payments and bribes	Average score across the five components of the following Executive Opinion Survey question: "How common is it for firms to make undocumented extra payments or bribes connected with (a) imports and exports; (b) public utilities; (c) annual tax payments; (d) awarding of public contracts and licenses; (e) obtaining favorable judicial decisions". 1 - Very Common ; 7 - Never occurs	World Economic Forum (Schwab and Sala-i-Martin, 2015[8])	The Executive Opinion Survey administered each year in over 140 economies by the World Economic Forum (Schwab and Sala-i-Martin, 2015[8]) captures the opinions of business leaders around the world on a broad range of topics for which data sources are scarce or, frequently, non-existent on a global scale. These indicators score from 1 to 7, with higher scores corresponding to better outcomes.
Intellectual property protection	Average score of the following Executive Opinion Survey question: "How would you rate intellectual property protection, including anticounterfeiting measures, in your country?" 1 - Very weak; 7 - Very strong		
Organised crime	Average score of the following Executive Opinion Survey question: "To what extent does		

	organized crime (mafia-oriented racketeering, extortion) impose costs on businesses?" 1 - To a great extent; 7 Not at all		
		Free-trade zones	
Number of firms operating in export processing zones	Estimates of the number of firms operating in export processing zones in 2013.	OECD/EUIPO (2018)[9]	Estimates of the number of FTZs are based on based on the World FTZ database (Yücer, Siroën and Archanskaia, 2014[10]).
		Production facilities	
Share of the manufacturing sector in value added	Share of the manufacturing sector in value added	World Bank Doing Business Data (World Bank, 2014[11])	-
Minimum wage	Minimum wage applicable to the worker assumed in the case study: a full-time cashier employee, age 19, with one year of work experience and not member of the labor union, unless membership is mandatory. Economies for which 0.00 is shown have no minimum wage in the private sector. (USD per month)	World Bank Doing Business Data - Labor Market Regulation (World Bank, 2014[11])	Doing Business studies the flexibility of regulation of employment, specifically as it relates to the areas of hiring, working hours and redundancy. Doing Business also measures several aspects of job quality. For more information see http://www.doingbusiness.org/data/exploretopics/labor-market-regulation
Annual paid leave per worker	Paid annual leave for a worker assumed in the case study: a full-time cashier employee, age 19, not member of the labor union, unless membership is mandatory. (in working days). Average for workers with 1, 5 and 10 years of tenure.	World Bank Doing Business Data - Labor Market Regulation (World Bank, 2014[11])	
		Logistic performance indicators	
Ability to track and trace consignments (1='low' to 5)	Logistics professionals' perception of the ability to track and trace consignments when shipping to the country, on a rating ranging from 1 (very low) to 5 (very high). Scores are averaged across all respondents.		
Competence and quality of logistics services	Logistics professionals' perception of country's overall level of competence and quality of logistics services (e.g. transport operators, customs brokers), on a rating ranging from 1 (very low) to 5 (very high). Scores are averaged across all respondents.	Logisitc Performance Index Surveys (World Bank and Turku School of Economics, 2018[13]).	The LPI is based on a worldwide survey of operators on the ground (global freight forwarders and express carriers), providing feedback on the logistics "friendliness" of the countries in which they operate and those with which they trade. They combine in-depth knowledge of the countries in which they operate with informed qualitative assessments of other countries where they trade and experience of global logistics environment. Feedback from operators is supplemented with quantitative data on the performance of key components of the logistics chain in the country of work.
Ease of arranging competitively priced shipments	Logistics professionals' perception of the ease of arranging competitively priced shipments to a country, on a rating ranging from 1 (very		

Indicator	Description	Source	Notes
	difficult) to 5 (very easy). Scores are averaged across all respondents		
Efficiency of customs clearance process	Logistics professionals' perception of the efficiency of country's customs clearance processes (i.e. speed, simplicity and predictability of formalities), on a rating ranging from 1 (very low) to 5 (very high). Scores are averaged across all respondents.		
Frequency with which shipments reach consignee within scheduled or expected time	Logistics professionals' perception of how often the shipments to assessed country reach the consignee within the scheduled or expected delivery time, on a rating ranging from 1 (hardly ever) to 5 (nearly always). Scores are averaged across all respondents.		
Quality of trade and transport-related infrastructures	Logistics professionals' perception of country's quality of trade and transport related infrastructure (e.g. ports, railroads, roads, information technology), on a rating ranging from 1 (very low) to 5 (very high). Scores are averaged across all respondents.	Logisitc Performance Index Surveys (World Bank and Turku School of Economics, 2018[13]).	The LPI is based on a worldwide survey of operators on the ground (global freight forwarders and express carriers), providing feedback on the logistics "friendliness" of the countries in which they operate and those with which they trade. Feedback from operators is supplemented with quantitative data on the performance of key components of the logistics chain in the country of work.

Trade faciltation policies and measures

Indicator	Description	Source	Notes
Information availability	Publication of trade information, including on Internet; transparency of required documentation; user manuals; available legislation; enquiry points. Values range from 0 to 2, where 2 represents the best performance that can be achieved		
Involvement of trade community	Structure for consultations with traders; established guidelines for consultations; publications of drafts; existence of notice-and-comment frameworks. Values range from 0 to 2, where 2 represents the best performance that can be achieved	OECD Trade Facilitation Indicators (OECD, 2018[15])	The OECD indicators cover the full spectrum of border procedures for 163 countries across income levels, geographical regions and development stages. Values are calculated on the basis of information in the TFIs database.
Advance rulings	Prior statements by the administration to requesting traders concerning the classification, origin,		

	valuation method, etc., applied to specific goods at the time of importation; the rules and process applied to such statements. Values range from 0 to 2, where 2 represents the best performance that can be achieved		
Appeal procedures	The possibility and modalities to appeal administrative decisions by border agencies. Values range from 0 to 2, where 2 represents the best performance that can be achieved		
Fees and charges	Disciplines on the fees and charges imposed on imports and exports; transparency and regular review of fees and charges; disciplines on transparency and implementation of penalties systems. Values range from 0 to 2, where 2 represents the best performance that can be achieved		
Formalities - documents	Acceptance of copies, simplification of trade documents; harmonisation in accordance with international standards. Values range from 0 to 2, where 2 represents the best performance that can be achieved.		
Formalities - automation	Electronic exchange of data; use of risk management; automated border procedures. Values range from 0 to 2, where 2 represents the best performance that can be achieved		
Formalities - procedures	Streamlining of border controls; single submission points for all required documentation (single windows); post-clearance audits; authorised economic operators. Values range from 0 to 2, where 2 represents the best performance that can be achieved.	OECD Trade Facilitation Indicators (OECD, 2018[15])	The OECD indicators cover the full spectrum of border procedures for 163 countries across income levels, geographical regions and development stages. Values are calculated on the basis of information in the TFIs database.
Border agency cooperation - internal	Control delegation to Customs authorities; co-operation between various border agencies of the		

	country. Values range from 0 to 2, where 2 represents the best performance that can be achieved
Border agency cooperation - external	Cooperation with neighbouring and third countries. Values range from 0 to 2, where 2 represents the best performance that can be achieved.

References

Kaufmann, D., A. Kraay and M. Mastruzzi (2010), *The Worldwide Governance Indicators: Methodology and Analytical Issues*, World Bank Policy Research Working Paper No. 5430, World Bank, Washington, DC, http://papers.ssrn.com/sol3/papers.cfm?abstract_id=1682130.

OECD (2018), *Trade Facilitation Indicators*, http://www.oecd.org/trade/facilitation/indicators.htm.

OECD/EUIPO (2018), *Trade in Counterfeit Goods and Free Trade Zones: Evidence from Recent Trends*, OECD Publishing, Paris/EUIPO, http://dx.doi.org/10.1787/9789264289550-en.

OECD/EUIPO (2017), *Mapping the Real Routes of Trade in Fake Goods*, OECD Publishing, Paris, http://dx.doi.org/10.1787/9789264278349-en.

OECD/EUIPO (2016), *Trade in Counterfeit and Pirated Goods: Mapping the Economic Impact*, OECD Publishing, Paris, http://dx.doi.org/10.1787/9789264252653-en.

Schwab, K. and X. Sala-i-Martin (2015), *The Global Competetiveness Report 2014-2015*, World Economic Forum.

World Bank (2014), *Doing Business Data*, World Bank, Washington, DC, http://www.doingbusiness.org/data.

World Bank and Turku School of Economics (2018), *Logistic Performance Index Surveys*, World Bank, Washington, DC, http://www.worldbank.org/lpi.

Yücer, A., J. Siroën and E. Archanskaia (2014), *World FTZ Database*, http://ftz.dauphine.fr (accessed on November 2017).

OECD PUBLISHING, 2, rue André-Pascal, 75775 PARIS CEDEX 16
(42 2018 30 1 P) ISBN 978-92-64-30245-7 – 2018